BUGGED

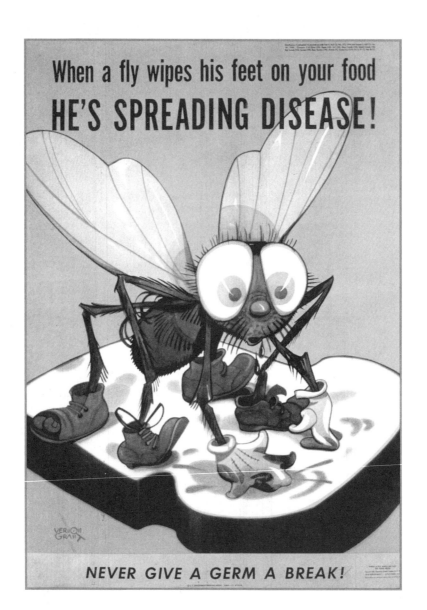

WITHDRAWN

BUGGED

HOW INSECTS CHANGED HISTORY

SARAH ALBEE

illustrated by
ROBERT LEIGHTON

BLOOMSBURY
NEW YORK LONDON NEW DELHI SYDNEY

First published in the United States of America in April 2014
by Walker Books for Young Readers, an imprint of Bloomsbury Publishing, Inc.
www.bloomsbury.com

Bloomsbury is a registered trademark of Bloomsbury Publishing Plc

For information about permission to reproduce selections from this book, write to
Permissions, Bloomsbury Children's Books, 1385 Broadway, New York, New York 10018
Bloomsbury books may be purchased for business or promotional use. For information on bulk purchases
please contact Macmillan Corporate and Premium Sales Department at specialmarkets@macmillan.com

Library of Congress Cataloging-in-Publication Data
Albee, Sarah.
Bugged : how insects changed history / by Sarah Albee.
p.   cm.
ISBN 978-0-8027-3422-8 (paperback) • ISBN 978-0-8027-3423-5 (reinforced)
1. Insects—History—Juvenile literature. 2. Human-animal relationships—History—Juvenile literature.
I. Title. II. Title: How insects changed history.
QL467.2.A43 2014   595.7—dc23   2013025968

Printed in China by Leo Paper Products, Heshan, Guangdong
4 6 8 10 9 7 5 3   (paperback)
2 4 6 8 10 9 7 5 3 (reinforced)

All papers used by Bloomsbury Publishing, Inc., are natural, recyclable products
made from wood grown in well-managed forests. The manufacturing processes
conform to the environmental regulations of the country of origin.

For Jon, Sam, Cassie, and Luke.
Sorry about all the bug talk at the dinner table.
—S. A.

For my father, who worked like the Ant and now
plays like the Grasshopper
—R. L.

Contents

Preface

THERE ARE ABOUT TEN QUINTILLION insects in the world. For as long as humans have been on earth, we have coexisted with insects, whether we liked it or not.

This book is about how insects have changed human history, for better or for worse. We're going to read about some of the most dangerous, coolest, and grossest bugs on the planet. And we're going to read about how they contributed to some of the most interesting, deadly, and shocking episodes in human history.

Even if you're a person who doesn't like bugs, you have to admit that it isn't fair to say a bug is good or bad. A hungry flea is just trying to get a bite to eat, a stinging bee is just trying to defend her home from invaders, and a dung beetle rolling a ball of poop is just trying to make a living. But we'll talk about bugs that have been good for *us*, like silkworms and honeybees, and bugs that have been very bad for us, like the ones that spread infectious diseases.

You'll also read a little bit here about the stinging, biting, and bloodsucking kinds of bugs, the ones most people are afraid of. But these human harassers will not be our focus. Because this is really a history book. And even though hornet stings really hurt, and even though it is extremely upsetting when you find yourself on the dinner menu of loathsome **parasites** like bedbugs or botflies or head lice, these unpleasant encounters with bugs haven't changed human history. (Bold-faced words appear in the Glossary.) No matter how traumatizing it may be for the person who gets bitten or stung or pinched, or who finds half a worm waving hello from his apple, these types of bugs don't usually spread infectious diseases.

Hollywood has made plenty of highly improbable horror movies involving man-eating **arthropods**, but in reality most insects won't bother you at all, and there are very, very few that can kill a person directly. (One notable exception would be when a person with a life-threatening allergy dies from a bee sting.) But there *are* species of insects that can kill a huge number of people *indirectly*. These insects transmit disease from animal to person (such as plague) or from person to person (such as malaria or yellow fever). The truly harmful bugs are those that cause indirect injury, and the diseases they've spread have changed the world.

Be very afraid . . . if you're a cricket.

DON'T SAY I DIDN'T WARN YOU

THIS BOOK IS FULL OF death, disease, and disgusting details about some of the most horrible events in human history. You may quickly grow numb to the disaster statistics. You'll read about bugs that can suck most of the blood out of your body; bugs that eat dead people; swarming, crop-crunching bugs that can darken the sky for days; and bugs that transmit diseases that make you blow up like a balloon, turn bright yellow, or cause worms to crawl through your body and then bore their way, slowly and painfully, out of your arm or leg. If you don't want to be grossed out, or you are easily scared, you should probably stop reading now and go check out a nice book about butterflies or something. If you do decide to continue reading, keep in mind that the grossest information appears under the headings "TMI" (Too Much Information), so if you're the squeamish sort, you can skip those.

To avoid making this book ten quintillion pages long, I had to flit through world history, mayfly-like, which was hard because so many topics are really fascinating and deserve more in-depth treatment. If you want to learn more about a particular insect or disease or period of history, please check out the Further Reading and Surfing section at the end of the book. I relied on the research of many historians and scientists, and I hope you'll go read their books.

A BIT OF BUG BIOLOGY

AND NOW FOR A LITTLE science. It might help you to know something about insect life cycles, scientific naming, and a few scientific terms, to better understand how bugs behave and evolve and metamorphose and spin cocoons and pollinate plants and transmit germs.

BABY BUGGIES

MOST NEWBORN INSECTS don't look anything like their parents. Although a few species are born live, most insects hatch from eggs.

You have probably already studied metamorphosis—a change from one form to another. But it may help to review, because throughout the book we'll be talking about insects at different phases in their life cycles. Most insects pass through four stages: egg, larva (also called maggot or grub or wriggler or caterpillar), chrysalis or pupa (which is encased in a cocoon), and adult. This four-step process is known as complete metamorphosis. Insects that go through complete metamorphosis include butterflies, moths, beetles, flies, fleas, mosquitoes, bees, wasps, and ants.

Some insects go through only three stages of metamorphosis: egg, nymph (a small version of the parent), and adult. This is known as incomplete metamorphosis. Grasshoppers, crickets, termites, mayflies, cockroaches, head lice, and dragonflies go through incomplete metamorphosis.

DON'T COME IN! I'M CHANGING!

CRAWLER ID

THROUGHOUT THIS BOOK, WE'LL REFER to most insects by their common names, such as ladybug, mosquito, and ant. But occasionally you'll see a two-part Latin name if we need to be specific. Every known living thing–from a microscopic bacterium to a giant blue whale–has a scientific name, which is how scientists know exactly what species someone's talking about. For instance, the species of mosquito that transmits yellow fever is called *Aedes aegypti*, which translates to "unpleasant Egyptian."

I've also referred to insects as bugs, which isn't technically accurate. True "bugs" are a small category of insect (including, for example, stinkbugs). But since practically everyone calls insects bugs, I've used that common term for all members of the class Insecta.

WHAT *IS* AN INSECT?

AN INSECT IS AN INVERTEBRATE, MEANING there are no bones inside its body. Most bugs have hard exoskeletons to protect their soft guts, which is why you may hear a grotesque cracking sound if you squish one. At some point in its life cycle, an insect has three parts to its body (head, thorax, abdomen) and six jointed legs.

Eight-legged spiders, ticks, and mites are not insects. They have neither the three-part body nor six legs, which kicks them out of the category.

So you won't be reading about Lyme disease here, because ticks transmit Lyme disease and ticks are not insects. And you won't be reading about giant, man-eating spiders, because (a) there's no such thing as giant, man-eating spiders, and (b) spiders aren't insects.

Not to worry—spiders aren't insects.

LET THE BEDBUGS "BITE"

ONE LAST NOTE—YOU'LL SEE A lot of talk about bugs that bite, but in fact, most bugs don't have the right mouthparts to clamp down and chomp away at you. A mosquito, for example, stabs you with her sharp, pointed proboscis and sucks up your blood while dripping a chemical into you that keeps your blood thin enough to get sucked up. But it's easier to say "bite" than the more technically accurate "stab with the proboscis and suck," don't you think?

1

The Insect Facts of Life

CAN'T LIVE WITH 'EM, CAN'T LIVE WITHOUT 'EM

NEARLY EVERYONE HAS A STRONG opinion about insects. But whether you love them or loathe them, you know they're impossible to avoid. For every pound of us, there are three hundred pounds of insects. And while most insects keep a pretty low profile, there are some that have a huge impact on our lives.

You may have noticed that bugs don't figure into history books much, and that the average history textbook ignores the collision of the insect world with the human world. This should shock you. Once you start looking at the world through fly-specked glasses, you'll start to realize how much these tiny life-forms have shaped human history.

Bugs have affected the outcome of nearly every war ever fought, because bugs carry diseases, including typhus, plague, cholera, yellow fever, malaria, typhoid, and dysentery. These diseases have killed a lot more soldiers than swords and guns have. Insects influenced the rise of Christianity, Buddhism, and Islam. They ended the Golden Age of Athens and helped topple the empires of ancient Rome, Byzantium, Alexander the Great, and Napoleon. As many as six of the ten plagues of Egypt in the Bible may have involved insects. Bugs have made nations rich and helped create vast empires. They've brought industries to a grinding halt, caused kingdoms to collapse, and set off widespread human famine.

Insects even led to the invention of the gin and tonic.

ENTOMOLOGY IS the study of insects—not to be confused with etymology, which is the study of words and where they come from.

INSECT ASIDE

SAME DIFF

INSECTS AND HUMANS have a lot more in common than you might think. Insects have jobs. They herd other insects the way we herd cattle. They live in well-organized societies. They form relationships. They enslave other insects. They wage war. They take out the garbage, make music, prepare food, and communicate with one another.

SURVIVAL OF THE FLITTIEST

INSECTS HAVE BEEN AROUND SINCE the Paleozoic era, which means they've been flying, scuttling, and hiding in corners for about four hundred million years. By the time modern-looking humans showed up—roughly 120,000 years ago—people were already sharing their bedding, homes, and bodies with many types of creepy-crawly insects.

Insects have the ability to reproduce in staggering numbers. One termite queen can produce hundreds of thousands of eggs in her lifetime. A large swarm of locusts might contain as many as ten *billion* insects. And though it might be easy to swat one fly or smash one mosquito, it's much harder to do away with an entire insect species, which has a remarkable ability to change as needed and not only survive but thrive. How do they do it?

It's a bird! It's a plane! It's . . . ten billion locusts!

For one thing, because they can produce huge numbers of offspring, insects ensure that at least some of their young are bound to survive. One type of aphid doesn't even need a male to reproduce; she just clones herself and produces more aphids.

For another, insects are small. Small bodies don't require much food. A flea can live 125 days without a meal. Insects' small size and flattened bodies also help them hide from their enemies, as anyone who has ever lived with roaches can tell you.

THE GOOD, THE BAD, AND THE UGGY

WE CAN'T LIVE WITHOUT INSECTS. THEY pollinate plants, recycle dead stuff, serve as food for other animals, till and enrich the soil, and perform all sorts of tasks most of us are entirely unaware of. The benefits we get from the majority of insects far outweigh the harm done by the few destructive ones. And yet, insects have caused a lot of human misery. They can be **vectors**—that is, transmitters—of some seriously deadly diseases.

Termites. They're what's for supper.

Why don't most people in the United States and Europe know much about these insect-transmitted diseases? First, insects pose a very small risk to our health, thanks to decent health care, temperate (nontropical) climate, good plumbing, and scientific knowledge of insects' breeding habits.

Second, diseases transmitted by insects tend to infect the poorest of the poor, in places where Western reporters don't go very often. In hot climates, insects are free to abuse, infect, and infest humans on a year-round basis. Insect-transmitted diseases often strike at the same time as natural and man-made disasters such as floods, earthquakes, and wars, so it can be hard to tell how much of the misery during these terrible events has been caused by insects.

And finally, many of the diseases insects carry don't actually kill people, or at least not right away. You can have malaria or intestinal parasites or Chagas' disease or typhoid for many years. But these diseases make a lot of people ill for a long time, and that means a huge number of the world's children grow up sickly and undernourished, and a huge number of adults are too weak to perform their jobs.

Think all of this is ancient history or happening far enough away that these insects won't affect you? Think again. Several diseases and pests once considered to be things of the past are now back and as deadly as ever. Although many of us have never experienced a terrible **epidemic**, that doesn't mean it couldn't happen. Those of us living in cooler climates, where many of the most dangerous insects can't survive the winter, tend to take disease-free living for granted. But climates are changing, and insects are continually evolving and adapting. Scientists are trying to stay ahead of these quick-change artists and the ever-evolving germs they carry, but it's a never-ending battle.

The Horrible History of Human Hygiene

HOW TO CATCH A BUG FROM A BUG

THERE ARE FOUR WAYS YOU can catch an infectious disease: by breathing germy air, touching someone—or something—with germs, drinking germy water, or getting bitten by a germ-carrying insect or animal. In ancient times, people knew about the air and touch ways. In fact, they thought these were the only ways you could catch a disease.

Before the end of the nineteenth century, if someone fell ill with what was believed to be a contagious disease (see Glossary box on Contagious versus Infectious), doctors usually told people to stay as far away as possible from that person, to avoid touching or breathing in the person's germs. People also avoided places that smelled bad—not so easy in the days before modern sanitation. Bad-smelling

Plague doctors wore heavy gowns for protection and beaked masks full of herbs to purify the air. They carried sticks to ward off sick people.

12

air, doctors believed, was full of poisonous vapors, known as miasmas, that shouldn't be breathed in. People thought you caught malaria from breathing in the vapors that floated up from swamps. The word "malaria" is Italian for "bad air."

Everyone assumed that the key to staying healthy was to avoid all contact with sick people. That's why people with leprosy had to carry bells everywhere they went (to warn others of their approach), why plague victims had their doors nailed shut (with them inside), and why ships carrying sick sailors had burning arrows fired at them (to prevent them from approaching a port town).

Today we know a lot more about how diseases are transmitted. We know now that people catch some diseases, like cholera and typhoid and dysentery, by drinking dirty water. You can't "catch"

Lepers were often required to ring bells to warn people of their presence.

these by being touched or coughed or sneezed on. And many other diseases—like malaria, bubonic plague, typhus, and yellow fever—are transmitted by bugs. These are the types of diseases we're going to be looking at in this book. The only way to catch them is if a bug bites an infected person or animal and then bites you.

INSECT ASIDE

NITPICKERS

BACK IN MEDIEVAL TIMES, people hired sharp-eyed, nimble-fingered women to pluck off their lice.

Nowadays panicked parents of lousy (louse-ridden, that is) schoolchildren hire professional nitpickers, who enjoy a thriving business. Today the term "nitpicker" means someone who focuses too closely on unimportant details.

POSSESSED OR JUST INFESTED?

BEFORE SCIENTISTS FINALLY DISCOVERED THE existence of germs, most people thought that epidemic diseases were caused by angry gods or planetary movements or enemies poisoning wells. Perfectly rational people believed in curses by demons, werewolves, witches, and leprechauns. It did not occur to most people that they could get sick by drinking filthy water or by being bitten by the insects that were crawling all over their bodies, clothing, and homes.

How could they not see that there might be a link between bugs and filth and catching a disease? Maybe because bugs and filth were a normal part of everyday life, even for rich people. It's hard for those of us living now to imagine, but throughout most of human history, city streets were piled with animal and people poop, waterways were reeking and polluted, and people—rich and poor alike—were quite literally crawling with bugs. Most people owned just one set of clothes, which were matted, patched, and filthy, and often these were passed along from one generation to the next.

Bugs have bugged people from the very beginning of recorded time. Mummified nits (louse eggs) have been found on combs in tombs from ancient Egypt. King Tut is now believed to have died from a severe case of malaria. Many wealthy ancient Romans plucked all the hair off their bodies, in part to prevent lice. Scientists examining fossilized Viking poop (now *that*'s a fun job) have discovered it to be full of fossilized parasites. In ancient South Asia, people bathed regularly, but the tropical river valleys they called home were swarming with insects, and the diseases transmitted by these insects—most notably malaria, plague, and cholera—killed untold numbers of people. In medieval Europe, people thought taking a bath was bad for you. Hardly anyone bathed, and as most clothing was not colorfast (meaning the dyes ran if the clothes got wet), people never washed their clothes. Lice and fleas were part of life.

DEAD MAN WALKING

IN 1170, the archbishop of Canterbury, Thomas à Becket, was murdered at Canterbury Cathedral. When people examined his body, they found Becket's clothes to be so full of fleas and lice that in the words of one witness, the dead man's robes "boiled over with them like water in a simmering cauldron."

Swarmed!

Scientists discovered that bugs can transmit diseases only about a hundred years ago. If you were to try to explain to a medieval physician that the cause of his patient's fever was a bug bite, he'd probably think you had lost your senses and would prescribe a hefty dose of mercury and a good bloodletting. (See There Will Be Blood box, page 62.)

3

The Land of Silk and Honey

BENEFICIAL BUGS

BAD BUGS GET A LOT of bad press, but it's important to remember that most insects steer clear of us. And others help us a lot. Unlike most chapters in this book, this one contains a minimum amount of unpleasantness and death.

Insects are an important source of food for animals all the way up the food chain. Where would birds and fish and anteaters be without bugs to eat? Insects also help us grow our food by pollinating most fruits, nuts, and vegetables. Your diet would be extremely dull without the help of pollinating insects.

Thank a bee.

And let's not forget the insects that decompose dead stuff. This is a very important job. If it weren't for these lowly little recyclers, we'd be wading through waste.

What other goods and services do insects provide for us humans? It's a long and impressive list, but here are just a few.

INSECT SPIT

SILK HAS BEEN A HIGHLY prized fabric for thousands of years. It's wrinkle resistant, comfortable, lightweight, and warm. It can be dyed deep and striking colors. It's the strongest natural fiber known. And who knew it was made from dried caterpillar spit?

As a matter of fact, no one knew, outside of China, for centuries. The Chinese guarded the secret of silk making for hundreds of years. Anyone caught leaking the secret could be executed.

Legend has it that around 2600 BC, the Chinese Empress Xi Ling Shi was sitting under a mulberry tree when a cocoon dropped into her teacup. Looking down, she saw a mass of shimmery strands floating in her cup, and they turned out to be one long, continuous thread.

All moths spin some sort of silky cocoon, but one species is a master at it: *Bombyx mori* can spin its goopy thread at a rate of six inches a minute. One cocoon can be drawn out into a continuous silken line a half mile long.

Spin doctors

INSECT ASIDE

THE VERY HUNGRY CATERPILLARS

SILKWORMS ARE FAMOUSLY FINICKY. The only thing they'll eat are the leaves of mulberry trees. And they don't like loud noise. Silk workers have to pad around in muffled shoes so as not to upset the silkworms.

SPIT AND POLISH

SCALE INSECTS ARE A HUGE group of various species. They look different from most insects. Small, immobile, with no legs, scale insects often look like fish scales. Many are destructive to plants. Some feed on sap, which can kill the plant. Others transmit diseases to plants—90 percent of all plant **viruses** are transmitted by scale insects. Fern scales and mealybugs are charter members of the group of scale insect pests. (See Parasites to the Rescue, page 141.)

But a few species of scale insects have been extremely helpful to humans. Shellac is made from a sticky goo secreted by certain types of *lac* insects that live in India and Burma (also known as Myanmar). Workers harvest the sticky lac secretion, then grind, soak, and stomp on it. After drying and bleaching in the sun, the lac is heated, stretched into thin sheets, and then broken into flakes. When you dissolve the flakes in alcohol, you get a varnish.

Yep, it's an insect. No, really.

BUFFED

SECRETIONS FROM LAC INSECTS can also be transformed into the shiny coatings on pills, candies, playing cards, and bowling alley lanes.

SEEING RED

WHEN THE SPANISH CONQUISTADOR HERNANDO Cortés first encountered the Aztecs of Mexico in 1518 (see Hernando Cortés, page 68) he was amazed by the brilliance of the red robes worn by the Aztec leader, Montezuma II, and his high-ranking officials. The color was brighter and richer than any red seen in Europe. Over the years, European cloth dyers and painters had tried to use all kinds of things to create a deep, vivid shade of red, including blood, bark, leaves, and dung. But none of these really worked—they produced an unsatisfying shade of pink or brownish rust. The best red dyers had been able to come up with had come from a type of insect called kermes, and the second-best came from a plant known as madder root.

Montezuma II

Cortés was doubly astonished when he learned that the Aztecs' brilliant red was made from squashed bug bodies.

Dactylopius coccus, otherwise known as cochineal, is a scale insect native to Mexico. It feeds only on a certain species of prickly pear cactus. Since the female can't fly

I TOLD YOU NOT TO SQUEEZE IT.

(she doesn't even have legs), she wards off predators by producing a bad-tasting red acid. If you squash the female insect, red gunk comes out.

After conquering the Aztecs, Cortés and his men seized several bags of the ground-up insects and sent them back to Spain. By 1587, as many as 75 tons of cochineal were shipped from Mexico to Spain.

Spain made a fortune producing and selling the red dye to the rest of the world. Cochineal quickly replaced kermes and madder as the red of choice for cardinals' robes, British officers' coats, and famous Renaissance painters' palettes. The Spanish guarded the secret closely and brutally—many Aztec workers employed in the dye-making business were murdered to keep the process a secret. Other countries turned to spying and piracy to try to figure out how the Spaniards did it. (See Sir Frances Drake, page 78.) Eventually French and Dutch spies managed to smuggle out some scale insects and begin making their own red dye. Cochineal production became a huge industry well into the nineteenth century, when synthetic fabric dyes were invented and became a cheaper alternative.

TOO MUCH INFORMATION? TMI

THERE REALLY IS A BUG IN MY SOUP

NEXT TIME YOU'RE AT THE GROCERY STORE, pestering your mom or dad for that strawberry ice cream, bright-red sports drink, or cherry-banana slurp-up yogurt, have a look at the list of ingredients on the package. If you see key words like "color added" or "carmine" or even "natural color," you might choose to rethink. Many foods and drinks that come in bright shades of red, orange, pink, and purple get their color from crushed bug carcasses. Cochineal is still used as a natural food coloring for many brands of ice cream, jelly, yogurt, cookies, chewing gum, and cough drops. It's also used to tint cosmetics like lipstick and blush.

INSECT ASIDE

HERS AND HERS

WORKER ANTS AND BEES—virtually every ant and bee that you see—are all female. Most male ants and bees live only a short time. They die soon after mating with the queen.

HOW SWEET IT IS

Helpful Honeybees

D O YOU SHUDDER TO THINK WHAT life was like before sugar? Actually, it wasn't as grim as you might think—people have been harvesting honey for thousands of years. Before sugar, honey was the world's only form of sweetener. And it's made by bees.

Honeybees flit from flower to flower collecting nectar. The honeybee returns to the hive with a stomach full of nectar, which she spits back up into a waxen cell (the honeycomb) and then mixes with more saliva. Other worker bees then fan the cell with their wings to get the water to evaporate faster. When the cell is full of concentrated honey, the bees cap it with wax, which they secrete from glands on the underside of their abdomen.

Since ancient times, people realized that both the honey and the wax were highly useful products. Beeswax has been used to embalm mummies and to make candles, cosmetics, batik fabric, and paints. It's still an ingredient in many cosmetics, shoe polishes, mustache wax, cheese rinds, and shaving creams.

Nice House, Nobody Home

A BOUT ONE-THIRD OF THE HUMAN DIET comes from bee-pollinated crops. Since 2006, honeybees have been mysteriously disappearing from their hives. As many as one-third of all the bee colonies in the United States may have vanished, and it's happening in other countries as well. The mass disappearance has become known as **Colony Collapse Disorder**. Scientists have been scrambling to figure out why. The evidence seems to be leaning toward a combination of factors. Some of the leading suspects include a parasitic mite, a fungus, a virus, toxic pesticides, and droughts. Other, unproven theories point to stress from overwork (due to beekeepers' extending the pollination season) or even vibrations from cell-phone towers.

Recently, a new threat facing honeybees has been identified. A parasitic phorid fly

Little zombie maker in action

(*Apocephalus borealis*) turns honeybees into zombies. The fly jumps on the bee's back and lays her eggs between the segments of the bee's abdomen. Soon, maggots hatch and start eating the bee from the inside out. Not surprisingly, this changes the bee's behavior, causing it to act strangely. She abandons the hive, becomes disoriented, and flies toward lights (something bees don't ordinarily do). After a few days, the maggots emerge, and the bee dies.

INSECTS AS FOOD

Pleased to Eat You

BUG EATING DOESN'T JUST HAPPEN on extreme reality shows. Insects are an important source of protein in many parts of the world, especially in places where chicken and steak can be hard to come by. Bugs have been a big part of many people's diets for centuries.

Crunchy and delicious

The ancient Greeks and Romans regularly ate insects. The Greeks chomped on toasted cicadas, whereas Romans favored softer beetle grubs.

According to the Bible, some leaping insects are actually kosher (Leviticus 11:21–22), including locusts, crickets, and grasshoppers. In Matthew 3:4, John the Baptist dines on locusts and honey.

People eat bug poop too. Honeydew is the sweet-tasting poop of aphids (not to be confused with the melon of the same name, which is a different food entirely). The Hebrew word for honeydew is *man*, and the "manna from heaven" that the Bible says kept the Israelites alive as they fled through the desert from Egypt is thought to have been aphid doo. Honeydew is still harvested in northern Iraq by the Kurds and is used to make a sweet confection. It's considered a delicious treat.

You can enjoy bugs roasted or raw; it's really a matter of personal preference. Some people like them alive and chewy, while others consider it a bit creepy to watch their dinner crawling off their plates and prefer them roasted or stewed. In Colombia, toasted ants are a common snack food. In China, deep-fried silkworm pupae are a delicacy. In Uganda, people crunch on live termites. In parts of Asia, giant water bugs are a common menu item. In Japan, fried grasshoppers are eaten with soy sauce, and in Peru, you can sample raw, living, wriggling, shiny white palm grubs—the guts squirt out in a burst of flavor as you bite down.

Be sure to try these regional dishes if you travel to these places.

Mmm!

BUG APPÉTIT

CHOCOLATE-COVERED CRICKETS

About 25 living, breathing, jumping crickets
3–4 ounces of semisweet chocolate

1. Rinse the live crickets in a colander. This is not as much fun as it sounds.
2. Put the clean crickets in a plastic bag and place them in the freezer until dead but not frozen solid (about fifteen minutes). If you like, remove heads and wings and legs. (The legs tend to get stuck in your teeth.)
3. Bake at 250 degrees until crunchy. (Cooking times may vary.)
4. Melt the chocolate in a double boiler, then dip each roasted cricket into the chocolate. Allow to set on waxed paper.

INSECTS AS MEDICINE

Larval Marvels

EVER WONDER WHY YOU OFTEN see flies buzzing around dead and decaying things? Some of them are laying their eggs. The larvae of these flies—you know them as maggots—will eat only dead tissue. Gross as that may sound to you, dead-tissue-eating maggots can be very helpful.

During World War I, two severely wounded soldiers were left for dead for several days on the battlefield. When they were finally brought in to the army hospital, doctors didn't believe the soldiers would live much longer. The soldiers' deep wounds were crawling with maggots. But before long, the doctors noticed that the maggots had cleaned the dead tissue better than any surgeon's knife could have. And the wounds were even beginning to heal, thanks to a natural antibiotic the larvae secrete that kills the **bacteria** in the wound and starts the healing process.

A World War I first-aid station

Maggots have been used to clean infected wounds for centuries by Aboriginal tribes in Australia, Burmese people, and Mayas in Central America. Now that some infections have proven to be resistant to antibiotics, "maggot therapy" is once again being used in the West.

This May Sting

BEE VENOM HAS BEEN USED as a medicine since ancient times and is growing in popularity in this country. It is used to treat patients suffering from many ailments, including arthritis, back pain, and skin conditions, probably because it contains melittin, which is an anti-inflammatory substance. The venom may be applied as a cream or injected. Or patients may pick up the bee with long tweezers and hold it next to their skin until the bee stings them. (Don't try this on your own.)

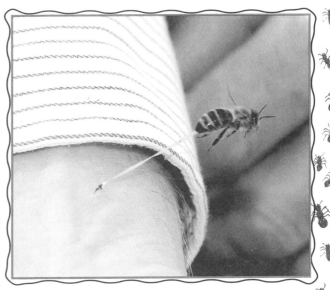

A rare image showing what happens when a bee stings a person

INSECT ASIDE — NO-BRAINER

YES, IT'S TRUE. A cockroach really can live without its head for weeks. It breathes through its body parts. Eventually it dies of starvation.

And the head of a cockroach may prove useful to modern medicine. Researchers have discovered that cockroach brains produce natural antibiotics that can kill off deadly bacteria. They're hoping to develop new medicines for humans using cockroach brain tissue.

HEY! GET BACK HERE!

Just a Spoonful of Honey

HONEY CONTAINS PLANT CHEMICALS THAT can prevent the growth of bad bacteria. It can kill antibiotic-resistant *Staphylococcus aureus*, which causes a serious infection and is often present in hospitals.

Suture Self

THE PRACTICE OF USING LARGE, biting ants to close wounds started in India about three thousand years ago and spread to other parts of the world. The wound would be held together while an ant was allowed to close its pincers over the edges of the wound. As its jaws closed down, the ant's head was twisted off, leaving its jaws in place. The clamped jaws acted as a stitch. Other ants would be put in place along the wound, holding it together until it healed. This must have hurt the wounded person a lot. (See Hey! Ouch! YEEEOWWWWW! box, page 36.) And it would also have caused serious problems for the ant.

FRISKY GENE POOL

FRUIT FLIES (*DROSOPHILA MELANOGASTER*) ARE a favorite insect of biologists. Fruit flies have made a huge contribution to the study of genetics. For one thing, they mature quickly. Twelve hours after they're born, they're cruising for mates. So researchers can observe changes from one generation to another over a relatively short period of time. They are not finicky eaters. Females can lay one hundred eggs a day. Most importantly, they share most of our genes. Although a nuisance buzzing around your fruit bowl, these tiny flies have led to big advances in the fields of biology and neuroscience.

INSECT DETECTIVES

REMEMBER THOSE SWARMING FLIES THAT laid eggs in open wounds from page 24? They also provide another service. As a dead body decomposes, different insect species move in, raise their families, and then move out again. The flitting flies, eggs, and larvae wriggling around inside dead bodies may sound disgusting, but they're of great interest to scientists who are known as forensic entomologists. These are the guys the police call when they find a dead body and want to know how long it's been there.

Blowflies, for instance, are very sensitive to the smell of decay. They also have extremely keen eyes and antennae and can spot a body when flying 115 feet above it. They can land on a corpse within minutes of death and may begin laying eggs right away. The resulting maggots may feed on the body for weeks.

Any body here?

After the maggots have developed into adult insects and flown away, other species move in until the body is almost completely devoured. Finally, certain kinds of moths and beetles polish off the skin, ligaments, and hair.

The sequence in which these insects appear is so predictable that it gives entomologists a very specific timeline. They can estimate the time of death and help solve crimes. They can often determine how many weeks or months have elapsed since death by examining which insects are in residence inside the body and where they are in their life cycles.

BEAUTY IS IN THE [COMPOUND] EYE OF THE BEHOLDER

NOT ONLY ARE MANY BUGS beneficial, but they can also be beautiful. Who doesn't love the sight of a colorful butterfly flitting among the flowers on a summer day? Or fireflies dancing in the air near a grove of trees at dusk? Or the sound of cicadas on a summer evening?

The ancient Egyptians worshipped dung beetles (also known as scarabs) as a symbol of resurrection and rebirth. Crickets have been kept as pets in China for thousands of years and are considered good luck. In Japan, dragonflies have long been symbols of courage and happiness and traditionally appear in paintings and poems. In parts of South America, live fireflies have been sewn into gauze and worn as decoration.

4
Bad-News Bugs

BUG THUGS: THE GANG OF FOUR

AS YOU KNOW BY NOW, MOST bugs don't bother us, and many do great things for us. But when bugs are bad, they are horrid. Four bad-news bugs in particular spread practically all insect-vectored diseases: the mosquito, the fly, the flea, and the louse. The diseases they transmit may be caused by a virus, bacteria, or **protist**.

BLOOD BANQUET

SMALL HERDS OF REINDEER living above the Arctic Circle have been found dead from exsanguination (having their blood sucked out), the result of swarms of mosquitoes and black flies.

Public Enemy Number One: Mosquito

NO ONE LIKES MOSQUITOES, AND HERE'S another reason not to: at least sixty species of these flying syringes can transmit serious diseases.

Only the female mosquito bites humans. She needs the protein in blood to form her eggs. As she sucks up a millionth of a gallon of a human's blood, she may inject **pathogens**, or germs, along with her saliva. These germs cause some terrible diseases.

Certain species of mosquitoes transmit malaria, which is one of the worst diseases ever to afflict humans (see Malaria box, below). Other mosquito-borne diseases include yellow fever, dengue (DEN-ghee), encephalitis (en-sef-uh-LY-tis), and West Nile virus (you'll read about all of these later).

POX BOX — MALARIA

MALARIA HAS BEEN A MAJOR HUMAN KILLER since caveman days, and the only way to get it is if a mosquito bites a sick person and then bites you. A person with malaria suffers from a high fever, which may occur and reoccur. A person may have daily attacks of fever every several days for as long as twenty years. But the more deadly strains can kill a victim within a matter of hours.

Public Enemy Number Two: Fly

THEY WALK OVER GARBAGE, POOP, and other decaying things, then walk on your food. And they don't wash their feet. They can carry germs on the hairs of their bodies and on their sticky feet, and spread them by touching, pooping on, or vomiting over your food.

Even the common housefly you see buzzing at your windowpane can be a serious health hazard, and flies of all species can transmit as many as sixty-five diseases. Major fly-vectored illnesses include sleeping sickness (see Sleeping Sickness box), Chagas' disease, guinea worm, river blindness, and leishmaniasis. (You'll read about the rest of these later.) Flies can also give you many other difficult-to-pronounce-let-alone-spell diseases, including dysentery, typhoid, cholera, poliomyelitis, typhus, tuberculosis, tutaraemia, anthrax, and spirochaetes. To add to the cheer, they can transmit pinworms, hookworms, and tapeworms.

POX BOX — SLEEPING SICKNESS

TRYPANOSOMIASIS, OR SLEEPING SICKNESS, is a disease transmitted by the bite of a tsetse fly. Pronounced "TSEE-zee," this large, blood-sucking fly lives only in Africa, along the riverbanks. Victims experience fever, chills, lethargy (sleepiness), enlarged liver and spleen, and disorientation. If the disease goes untreated, the victim usually dies within a year. The fly can also give the disease to animals, including cows and horses.

Public Enemy Number Three: Flea

FLEAS HAVE PLAGUED PEOPLE SINCE ancient times, but certain kinds of fleas can transmit *the* plague. (See Plague box, below.) Fleas can also give you deadly typhus.

PLAGUE

THERE ARE THREE KINDS OF PLAGUE, and two are transmitted by fleas. *Bubonic* plague is transmitted by the Oriental rat flea, which sucks up the bacteria *Yersinia pestis* from its dead or dying rat host. If there aren't any more rats available, the flea may settle for a human, where it regurgitates the bacteria into its new host.

About six days after a person is bitten by a diseased flea, symptoms appear. Untreated victims develop painful buboes (large lumps), which swell, harden, and turn black (hence the nickname "Black Death"). In severe cases, the lumps can burst.

During a terrible outbreak in the fourteenth century (see Fear and Fever in the Fourteenth Century, page 56), when the disease was especially deadly, victims vomited blood, and their skin blackened from internal bleeding. Tissue death—called necrosis—often occurred in the nose, fingers, toes, and other body parts. Sometimes bits and pieces of people fell off before they died in agonizing pain, as horrible smells arose from their rotting bodies.

Septicemic plague enters the bloodstream either through a flea bite or through a break in the skin, like a cut. The disease rapidly overwhelms the victim and, before antibiotics were developed, used to kill practically everyone who got it.

Pneumonic plague is not transmitted by fleas but rather through the air (by coughing or sneezing). The death rate is close to 100 percent if left untreated.

Some historians believe that during the world's worst plague **pandemics**, the bubonic plague changed to the pneumonic form, which led to the rapid and massive numbers of deaths (see The First of the Worst, page 50, and Fleas and Disease, page 83).

Nowadays all forms of plague can be treated with drugs if caught in time.

Public Enemy Number Four: Louse

DISCOVERING CREEPY-CRAWLY BUGS IN YOUR hair is a deeply unpleasant moment, as you know if you've ever had the misfortune to experience a case of head lice. But however unnerving it is to find them in your hair, head lice tend not to transmit serious diseases. It's body lice (also known as cooties) that do the most harm to humans. (See Typhus box, below.)

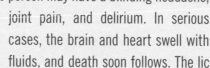

TYPHUS

TYPHUS IS A BACTERIAL DISEASE that has killed millions upon millions of people. The more fatal version, epidemic typhus, is transmitted by body lice or, less often, by fleas. It's not the bite but the feces of the insect that transmits the disease. The louse poop gets rubbed into a small break in the skin, which can happen when a person scratches a bite. A person can also become infected by breathing in the dust of dried lice poop.

Usually the victim develops a raging fever and a rash on the chest that spreads to the rest of the body. For a week or so, the person may have a blinding headache, joint pain, and delirium. In serious cases, the brain and heart swell with fluids, and death soon follows. The lice don't like their host to be too hot (that is, feverish) or too cold (that is, dead), so when that happens, they crawl off to find a new host, which is how the disease spreads.

Typhus becomes deadly in situations when people live in close quarters with one another and can't keep themselves clean, such as on ships or in prisons, concentration or refugee camps, and soldiers' trenches. Other names for epidemic typhus include ship fever, famine fever, and jail fever.

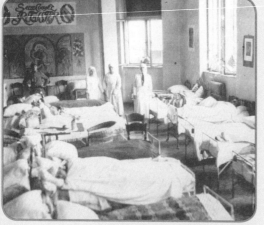
Typhus ward—Poland, circa 1920

HURLING HIVES

WARRING ENEMIES HAVE LOBBED buzzing beehive bombs at one another since ancient times. In ancient Rome, bees and hornets were placed inside large (breakable) clay urns and catapulted onto the decks of enemy ships. And as their enemies dug tunnels beneath their walls, besieged Romans drilled down and dropped swarms of furious stinging insects into the midst of their tunneling enemies.

The Mayas in Central America used bee booby traps to trick invaders. They hid beehives inside large gourds and created dummy warriors. They'd put war bonnets on the gourds and prop the dummies on the walls of their fortresses. When attackers scaled the walls, the Mayas burst the gourds and attackers would be swarmed with stinging bees, wasps, and biting flies.

Bees, wasps, and other stinging creatures were a favorite defense weapon during medieval times. Defenders of a castle dropped nests from the parapets, sending attackers into panicked retreat in a cloud of furious stinging hornets.

CROP CRUNCHERS AND OTHER BUGS THAT BUG US

IN ADDITION TO THE GANG OF FOUR, our rogues' gallery also includes bugs that can cause major damage to sources of human food. Agricultural pests can trigger crop failures and famines, which can result in huge numbers of people dying of starvation or finding themselves forced to move to new places. This group of crop crunchers includes locusts and mealybugs and boll weevils—all of which you'll read about later on.

BEETLE JUICE

EFFECTIVE POISONS HAVE ALWAYS BEEN IN DEMAND by second-born sons, impatient heirs, and people nursing grudges. In ancient India, poison makers discovered a highly toxic blister beetle and enjoyed a thriving business. The beetle's guts were so toxic that contact with the skin raised painful blisters, and contact with the eyes caused blindness. Applied to the point of a dagger, the poison could enter the bloodstream, where it would be more deadly than the bite of a cobra.

Do not smoosh!

What's Eating Him?

EVEN WHEN THEY DON'T TRANSMIT diseases, biting flies have determined where people settle, or don't. They have affected the movement of nomadic tribes. They drive away tourists, they discourage farmers, and they prevent people from setting up businesses.

Have a look at a map of Canada. Notice how huge sections of it are just blocks of map color, with few roads, no towns, and no cities? One major reason that so few people settled in the forested regions of the Canadian north is due to the presence

of biting insects—namely, black flies and mosquitoes. They're so bad that escaped prisoners hiding in the woods have turned themselves in, unable to withstand the maddening swarms of biting insects.

Researchers estimated that an unprotected person in the Canadian arctic could have half his blood drained by biting insects in about two hours. In the same study, Canadian scientists working near the Arctic Circle wanted to find out how many bug bites they would get in one minute of exposure. They averaged about nine thousand bites per person. *In one minute.*

HEY! OUCH! YEEE*OWWWWW!*

A RESEARCHER NAMED JUSTIN SCHMIDT got stung by a lot of bees, ants, and wasps in the course of his work. He and his colleagues developed the Schmidt Sting Pain Index and rated the painfulness of stings of seventy-eight species of insects, ranging from one ("a tiny spark") to four ("You might as well just lie down and scream").

Schmidt describes the sting of a fire ant, for example, as "sharp, sudden, mildly alarming—like walking across a shag carpet and reaching for the light switch." Moving higher up the pain scale, a bullhorn ant's sting feels like "someone has fired a staple into your cheek." A southern paper wasp's sting (shown right) is "like spilling a beaker of hydrochloric acid on a paper cut," and a bullet ant's sting is "pure intense brilliant pain, like walking over flaming charcoal with a three-inch nail in your heel."

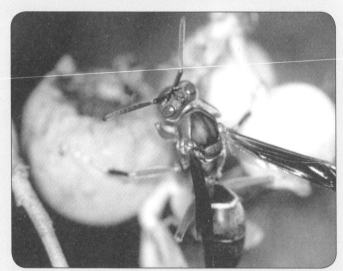

FLY BALL

MAYFLIES LIVE AS NYMPHS for several months to two years (depending on the species), but many of the adults usually live for only one day. Dead mayflies have been known to pile up on bridges like a snowfall. In July 2006, a huge cloud of mayflies that had hatched from the Mississippi River showed up on weather radar. A few hours later, bridges had to be closed while dead mayflies were removed with snowplows.

In October 2007, a Major League Baseball game between the New York Yankees and the Cleveland Indians was swarmed by clouds of mayflies in the eighth inning. Coughing and spitting out bugs, the Yankee pitcher, Joba Chamberlain, threw two wild pitches and walked a batter, which probably cost the Yankees the game.

The Earliest Epidemics

SETTLE DOWN!

BACK IN THE DAYS WHEN small bands of hunter-gatherers were always on the move following herds of animals, life was reasonably disease-free. People didn't stick around places long enough to foul the drinking water or let their waste pile up, so waterborne and insect-borne diseases weren't a big problem. Our early ancestors were more likely to die from accidents or wounds than from disease.

Insect troubles began about six thousand years ago, when people began to settle down, tame animals, and grow stuff. Insects settled down with them.

As populations grew bigger and bigger, insects evolved right alongside them. Farmers cleared land and cut down trees, disrupting the balance of nature, driving away insect-eating birds, and fertilizing with smelly organic matter, which created new breeding grounds for insects. The invention of irrigation produced puddles of standing water where bugs could lay eggs. As people produced more and more food, they began to store their excess grain. Moths and weevils and other stored-grain pests moved in too. Insects caused blights and fungi in the fields people had planted, resulting in terrible famines. Domesticated animals produced dung, as did their stay-at-home human owners, and that attracted a whole other vast and nasty collection of disease-bearing bugs.

INSECT ASIDE — EGG-DROP GOOP

MOSQUITOES LAY THEIR EGGS IN WATER. Mosquito larvae are champion swimmers. That's why swampy areas are great baby nurseries for mosquitoes and for the malaria parasite they may carry. Mosquitoes may also lay their eggs in puddles, rain barrels, and any small containers of standing water.

IT'S GETTING CROWDED

WHEN PEOPLE LIVED IN SMALL, isolated villages, diseases might race through and kill most of the people in the village, but that would be that. Settlements were far enough apart, and travel was difficult and infrequent enough, that diseases tended not to spread from place to place. But when cities formed, and filth and garbage piled up, insects and germs multiplied quickly. Unwashed people attracted lice. Filthy homes attracted rats and fleas. Poorly drained streets attracted mosquitoes. And open cisterns attracted flies. Droves of city dwellers in the ancient world died of insect-borne diseases like plague, typhus, yellow fever, typhoid, and malaria (see Chapter Four), as well as other contagious diseases like smallpox and influenza. These became known as crowd diseases. Crowd diseases require humans living crammed together in order to be able to spread from person to person.

It's rare in this day and age for massive numbers of people to die from a disease. But imagine if you lived in modern-day New York City and suddenly ten thousand people a day began dying of an unknown disease. What would you do?

Your first instinct might be to leave town. (That's what most people in the ancient world tried to do, at least those who could afford to.) But most likely, residents of the nearby towns of Scarsdale or Pelham or Hackensack wouldn't be very happy to see you, knowing you'd just left a place where an epidemic was raging. (That's how neighboring townspeople in the ancient world felt too.) Before they knew how diseases were spread, people assumed that standing close to a sick person would make them sick too. (This is not necessarily true; see Glossary, Contagious versus Infectious box.)

More often than not, when major diseases struck a city, people had nowhere to go, no means to help sufferers, and no idea how to stop the disease until it had run its awful course and killed off a large percentage of the population. Afterward, people were either dead or immune.

THE DREADED SPREAD

THE WORST EPIDEMICS IN HISTORY occurred when groups of people traveled to a new place and brought their insects and germs along with them. Sometimes they traveled by choice (see Deplorable Explorers, page 68), and sometimes very much not by choice (see Workers in Chains, page 72). The newcomers introduced their germs to native people who had never been exposed to those germs. The outcome was often disastrous. Native people's immune systems tried to fight off the unknown diseases by producing high fevers, rashes, vomiting, diarrhea, or buboes. You'll find multiple examples of these epidemics as you read on.

Over the course of time, as humans and their germs adapted to one another, some diseases became somewhat less deadly. Sometimes this downgrade took a few generations. Sometimes it took a few centuries. But eventually some insect-borne diseases became milder versions of their once-deadly forms—they became **endemic** (see Bantu Power, page 76). How did this happen? Children who didn't die from a disease grew up to be adults with resistance or **immunity** to that disease. These immune adults then had children, and that immunity was often passed on to their children. Chicken pox, for instance, has become a relatively mild childhood disease in the United States. But in times past, it was a major killer.

WHO KNEW? DIAGNOSING DISEASES

I**T CAN BE HARD ENOUGH TO** figure out what's wrong with a patient when the patient is right in front of you. It's a lot harder to figure out the nature of a disease that happened centuries ago. All we have to go on are accounts written by people living at the time. And to make it even more complicated, many ancient diseases may not look quite the same as their modern versions.

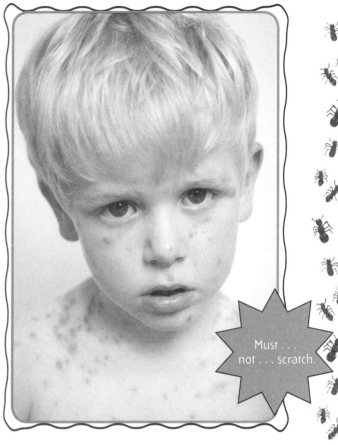

Must . . . not . . . scratch.

Descriptions in books written long ago that talk about "putrid fever" and "pernicious ague" and "grippe" and "flux" and "brain mould" make it hard to know for sure what actually ailed people. But based on what we know now about diseases, we can make educated guesses.

6

Close Encounters of the Ancient Kind

ANCIENT AILMENTS

BRACE YOURSELF. THERE'S A LOT of death and dying in this chapter. When epidemics struck people in the ancient world, bodies piled up fast.

Ancient Sanskrit and Chinese documents mention a disease that sounds like malaria, which ravaged the warmer, wetter parts of ancient China and India. In ancient India, people worshipped the fever demon Takman, and in ancient Rome, people prayed to the demon goddess of malaria, named Febris, for relief. Malaria was probably also a major killer in Babylon, Egypt, and Mesopotamia.

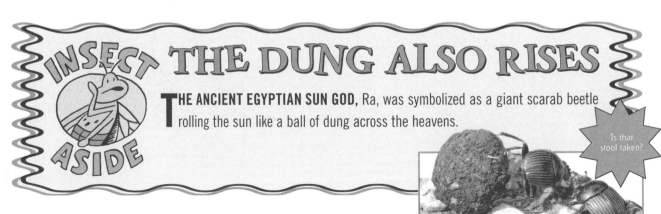

INSECT ASIDE — THE DUNG ALSO RISES

THE ANCIENT EGYPTIAN SUN GOD, Ra, was symbolized as a giant scarab beetle rolling the sun like a ball of dung across the heavens.

Is that stool taken?

BIBLICAL BUGS: HOLY TERRORS

AROUND THE END OF THE late Bronze Age (approximately 1200 BC), a fierce warring tribe of people came from the general direction of Greece or Cyprus and moved into Canaan, a land that covers parts of modern-day Egypt, Lebanon, and Israel. In the Bible they're known as the Philistines.

The Philistines wasted little time in swooping down upon the Israelites and conquering them. But their victory was short-lived. Almost immediately, the Philistines were struck by a terrible disease. As many as thirty thousand of them died.

An epic epidemic

To the victors go the germs—as shown in this seventeenth-century version of the Philistine plague.

Medical historians are still debating what the Philistine disease could have been. According to the account in the Bible, the Philistines were struck "with emerods in their secret parts" (1 Samuel 5:6). Now, we're not certain what an emerod is. Some people think it's a hemorrhoid, but although embarrassing and uncomfortable, hemorrhoids would not have caused so many deaths. It may also be translated as a swelling, so it seems more likely that the emerods the Philistines suffered from were buboes, and that the disease was bubonic plague. Realizing the Philistines were now weakened by disease, the Israelites seized the opportunity to fight back.

After the worst of the plague had passed, and still reeling from the horror the disease had caused, the Philistines decided it was time to wrap things up. They proposed that a pair of champions, one from each side, should duke it out to decide the war's outcome. The biblical story of David and Goliath recounts how the young Israelite boy, David, whups the strongest Philistine warrior, Goliath, by beaning him in the head with a stone fired from his sling. It makes for a great story, of course, but the Israelites' come-from-behind victory was most likely aided by a bunch of diseased fleas.

DELIRIOUS IN ASSYRIA

A FEW CENTURIES LATER, THE ASSYRIAN Empire ruled the ancient world. The Assyrians did invent some useful things, like keys, paved roads, the postal system, libraries, and the seven-day week. But they're better remembered for their brutal warfare. Their tendency to torture and slaughter huge groups of people whose lands they invaded made the Assyrians quite unpopular among their neighbors.

During one particularly murderous rampage, the Assyrian king, Sennacherib, sacked and burned Babylon. With the blood on his mens' swords not yet dry, he headed over to the city of Jerusalem to conquer the Judeans, who were cowering inside the walls of the city. But Sennacherib had barely begun besieging that city, in 701 BC, when he and his men suddenly packed up and left.

The question is, why?

Sennacherib—not much of a people person.

According to the Bible, an angel of the Lord came down and "slew in the camp of the Assyrians one hundred and eighty-five thousand" overnight (Isaiah 37:36). To put it in less poetic terms, a huge bunch of Sennacherib's soldiers began dying. It might have been plague, or possibly cholera.

Whatever the real cause, Sennacherib's army moved on and left the tiny kingdom of Judea alone. However unwittingly, Sennacherib allowed the kingdom to survive and flourish. As a result, the Judeans—and their Jewish religion—were able to evolve and thrive. Eventually it would branch into Christianity and Islam.

Sennacherib's retreat from Jerusalem changed the course of history and led to the rise of three major religions. Diseased fleas or flitting flies had once more changed the world.

PLAGUED WITH PESTS: THE ANCIENT GREEKS

AROUND 450 BC, ATHENS WAS the most important city (actually, city-state) in the world, and the center of culture, learning, art, and architecture. It was also an extremely crowded, dirty, smelly place.

In 431 BC, just when Athens was at the height of its power, war broke out between Athens and Sparta. Sparta, as you may know, was the second-most powerful city-state, where children were trained from early childhood to be warriors and where a Spartan's idea of a get-up-and-go breakfast was black soup, made from pig blood. Other city-states joined Sparta against Athens, and the Peloponnesian War, as it came to be called, dragged on for twenty-seven years, until everyone was either exhausted or dead.

FINISH YOUR PIG'S BLOOD, KIDS—

YOU'LL BE LATE FOR WAR.

Both sides fought savagely. In 430 BC, the Spartans laid **siege** to Athens. Huddled inside the already-crowded city, huge numbers of Athenians began dying from a strange and terrible plague. It killed their leader, Pericles. According to Thucydides, a Greek writer of the time who caught but managed to survive the disease, people developed a high fever and a "bloody tongue," and soon were coughing and vomiting—eventually leading to other symptoms too gross to mention even for this book—before they dropped dead.

The mysterious disease killed off about a quarter of the Athenian army and perhaps a third of the population of Athens. The war dragged on until Athens finally surrendered in 404 BC.

Modern scientists have studied the DNA from ancient remains to try to determine what it was that killed all those Athenians. But the nature of the disease is still a subject of lively debate. It may have been an early form of typhoid, typhus, measles, smallpox, or bubonic plague. Three out of five of these diseases are spread by insects.

The exhausted Spartans didn't have much time to celebrate their victory. The Macedonians, a tribe from the mountains north of Greece, swept in during the chaos that followed the war and conquered them.

Pericles

YOU DON'T SAY

"I am dying with the help of too many physicians."
—Alexander the Great

ALEXANDER THE GREAT-BIG-BULLY

ALEXANDER THE GREAT (356–323 BC) was a power-hungry Macedonian general and a serious egomaniac. As a young adult, he conquered most of the known world, including Persia, Syria, Phoenicia, Arabia, Egypt, most of the eastern Mediterranean coastline, and a good part of northern India. He built cities all over his empire and named a lot of them after himself. The most well-known today is Alexandria, Egypt.

In 323 BC, at the height of his power, the thirty-three-year-old general came down with a fever, lapsed into a coma, and died. Many historians think he died of malaria. If so, then a tiny mosquito took down one of the most powerful men who ever lived.

After his death, his empire collapsed and was eventually conquered by the Romans.

Alexander, wearing an awesome yet inauthentic hat

THERE'S NO PLACE LIKE ROME . . . UM, EXCEPT FOR CHINA

YOU PROBABLY KNOW AT LEAST something about ancient Rome (bread and circuses, gladiators, Julius Caesar, Emperor Nero, Pompeii), but did you know that another huge empire existed at the same time in a different part of the world? That would be the Han Dynasty, which ruled China from 202 BC until AD 220. Both empires had massive populations—in AD 14, Imperial Rome had about 54 million people; Han China, about 57 million. And the bustling trade between these two empires led to the spread of new and deadly epidemics.

The Chinese produced all of the world's silk (see Insect Spit, page 17), and the Romans were crazy about silk. In 126 BC, Emperor Wu Ti opened a six-thousand-mile trade route between China and Rome, by way of Turkestan and Iran. The route became known as the Silk Road. The Silk Road wasn't one particular road; it was an enormous trade network where silk, spices, and precious stones were traded. And as goods passed from one middleman to another, so too did germs, insects, and diseases.

China suffered two major outbreaks of some sort of plague-like epidemic, first in AD 161 and then in AD 310. But the population recovered and continued to expand and grow. Rome fared worse, as we will see.

THE EMPIRE SWATS BACK

ANCIENT ROME WAS NOT A healthy place if you happened to be a gladiator or a slave or even just someone with the misfortune to peek out from an upper-story window as the Emperor Caligula passed by. (He didn't want people to see his bald spot, so he made it a crime punishable by death to look down on him from above.) As time went on, Rome became an unhealthy place for just about anyone.

Again and again, major infectious diseases swept through the Roman Empire. An especially bad one struck in AD 251, killing as many as five thousand people a day. The disease did not kill just Romans. Thousands of foreigners were continuously streaming into the city, mostly people who had been captured from conquered territories and brought back to Rome as slaves. With so many people lacking immunity to diseases, huge numbers of people died.

Nice comb-over, Caligula

The timing of that epidemic, which may have been bubonic plague, probably helped Christianity gain some traction. More and more people converted to Christianity, perhaps assuming they were doomed and lured by the promise of a heavenly afterlife. An early Christian named Cyprian performed mass conversions of terrified people to Christianity. The epidemic became known as the plague of Cyprian.

More types of diseases followed. Although the Romans had suffered from malaria for centuries, many scientists are convinced that the disease took a dark turn and went from a troublesome summer illness to a deadly year-round problem.

Reeling from diseases and attacks by "barbarians" and devastated by famine caused by crop-crunching bugs, the Roman Empire split into two parts, forming an east and a west empire. In AD 312, Emperor Constantine—a convert to Christianity—moved the capital of the Roman Empire to the town of Byzantium, on the Black Sea in what is present-day Turkey. He renamed it Constantinople. (Today it's known as Istanbul.) It would grow into the glittering Byzantine Empire.

ASIAN INVASION

AROUND AD 370, FIERCE NOMADS from central Asia, known as the Huns, thundered across Europe, creating a swath of death and destruction. The terrorized people who managed to avoid being killed by the Huns—mostly tribes of Germanic people—hurried west into the Roman Empire, bringing their insect-borne diseases with them.

The Romans permitted some of these tribes to stay, and to hang on to their weapons, in a frantic bargain to help fend off the Huns. Tactical error? Probably, but the Romans were desperate. Forty years later one of those tribes, the Visigoths, attacked Rome and nearly destroyed it. But before it was completely flattened, the Visigoth king, Alaric I, died of a sudden fever, which seems likely to have been malaria.

HUNNY, I SHRUNK THE EMPIRE!

THE COMMANDER OF THE HUNS in AD 452 was a man named Attila, whose nickname became "Scourge of God." He was so feared that most rulers whose towns and cities he approached opened their wallets and paid him on sight, simply to ensure he wouldn't attack them. Attila and his well-disciplined men made it all the way to the very gates of Rome. Had they gone ahead and destroyed it, the course of history would have taken a rather dramatic turn. But something stopped them.

To the astonishment of everyone involved, Attila turned his army around and galloped right back out of Rome. Some historians credit Pope Leo I for bravely clambering over the Alps, seeking out Attila, and begging him to spare the city. But the more credible theory for why Attila turned around and left was that his army was weakened and devastated by disease. It's much more likely that mosquitoes, not the pope, saved Rome from the Huns' arrows.

A few years later, in AD 455, the Vandals finally sacked what remained of Rome. Severely weakened by diseases and unable to withstand the one-two punch of Visigoths and Vandals, Rome fell.

THE FIRST OF THE WORST

IN THE PAST TWO THOUSAND YEARS of human history, three major plague **pandemics** have struck the world. The first occurred during the reign of Emperor Justinian, who ruled Constantinople from AD 483 to 565. (For the second and third, read on.)

This plague of Justinian, as it came to be called, killed huge numbers of people. The sickness started with a high fever. After a day or two, painful egg-size lumps appeared on the neck,

Emperor Justinian (center)

armpit, or groin. Often hallucinations set in. More than half the victims died after five days. Was it bubonic plague? Many people think so, but medical historians believe it may have changed to the airborne version, pneumonic plague, which is close to 100 percent fatal (see Plague box, page 31). At the peak of the epidemic, as many as *ten thousand* people were dying each day.

They ran out of places to put the dead. Bodies were stacked inside houses or lugged aboard ships and sent to sea. The stench was overwhelming; the city was in chaos.

The plague spread across Europe and then to North Africa and the Middle East. It traveled eastward to Persia, Arabia, India, and, by 610, China, where it killed vast numbers of people and reappeared on and off for the next two hundred years.

By the time the Justinian plague finally ended, possibly *half* of the population of

Europe was dead. Even if they had known that bugs were to blame—and they didn't—people probably couldn't have done much to avoid the disease. This was a time before bug spray, before proper waste treatment and sewer systems, and before running water was available to the average person for bathing.

Because so many city dwellers had fled or died, most cities had far fewer people in them. A lot of people who had fled the cities stayed in the countryside. Demoralized, God-fearing, and dispersed, the population of Europe plunged into the Dark Ages.

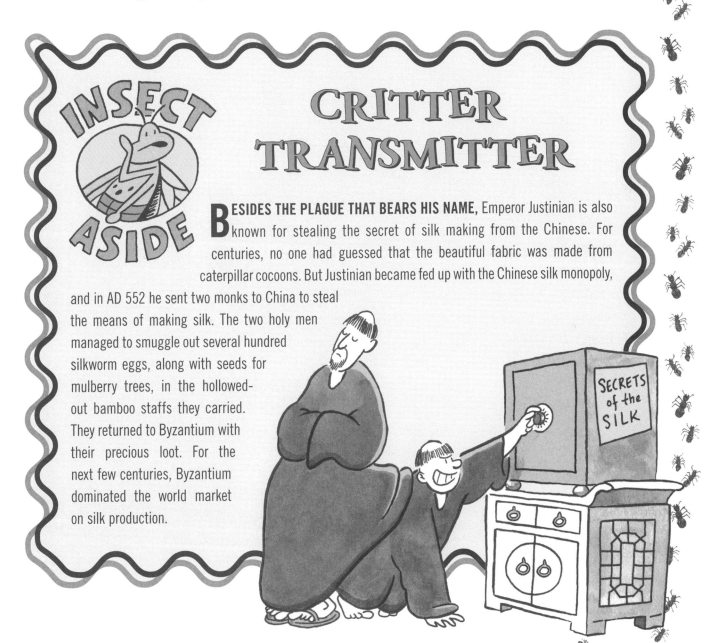

INSECT ASIDE

CRITTER TRANSMITTER

BESIDES THE PLAGUE THAT BEARS HIS NAME, Emperor Justinian is also known for stealing the secret of silk making from the Chinese. For centuries, no one had guessed that the beautiful fabric was made from caterpillar cocoons. But Justinian became fed up with the Chinese silk monopoly, and in AD 552 he sent two monks to China to steal the means of making silk. The two holy men managed to smuggle out several hundred silkworm eggs, along with seeds for mulberry trees, in the hollowed-out bamboo staffs they carried. They returned to Byzantium with their precious loot. For the next few centuries, Byzantium dominated the world market on silk production.

SECRETS of the SILK

7
Medieval Microbes

SCRATCH AND SNIFF

YOU'VE PROBABLY HEARD OF THE so-called Dark Ages, also known as medieval times, also known as the Middle Ages. It was a period of about a thousand years—roughly AD 500 to AD 1500—during which "the whole world" plunged for centuries into gloom, warfare, and ignorance. Much of the learning and art of the ancients was lost, allegedly destroyed by barbarians.

Actually, there are two sides to this story.

Most of the information we have about the "barbarians" (people thought to be uncivilized, uneducated, and primitive) was written by Romans, who considered any non-Roman to be uncivilized, uneducated, and primitive. And many Roman writers were unaware, or uninterested, in what was happening in Islamic and Asian kingdoms, where knowledge and learning continued to thrive. In fact, lucky for us, it turned out later that in these kingdoms, scholars preserved many of the books and writings of the ancient Greeks and Romans.

But it's certainly true that in Europe during this long period,

A captive from Dacia, conquered by
the Romans in the second century

hardly anyone bathed. Insects were a part of life. With nonexistent sanitation, constant warfare, and a society that provided little help for the poor, the old, or the sick, it's no wonder life was hard and short. But what's notable about the beginning of the Middle Ages is the absence of major epidemics. How could this be?

A rare bath

CLIMATE CONTROL

URING THE MIDDLE AGES, THE center of power shifted away from the hot, buggy Mediterranean cities of ancient times (Rome, Athens, Alexandria, Jerusalem) and moved north to areas with colder climates (France, England, Germany). Could bug-borne diseases have caused the shift north? It's certainly true that for many centuries, medieval Europeans suffered from fewer insect-borne diseases than had their predecessors in more southerly places.

Another factor that prevented major epidemics, at least at first, was that populations of medieval European cities didn't come close to the size of cities of ancient times. Villages were small, often with fifty or fewer inhabitants, and spaced far apart. Roads were rutted and muddy and dangerous, so people rarely ventured far from home. Infectious diseases simply had little opportunity to spread.

It took a few hundred years, but after Rome fell, European populations had a chance to bounce back from the terrible plagues of the fifth and sixth centuries. Nearly five hundred years went by without a major pandemic. It was only when people started to travel again (see Cruddy Crusaders, page 54) that epidemic diseases reemerged.

CRUDDY CRUSADERS

THE CRUSADES WERE A SERIES of bloody holy wars between Christians and Muslims, which were fought between 1099 and 1212. The pope called for Christians to travel to the Holy Lands and defend Christian holy places from the "infidels." And a lot of Christians answered the call. Peasants leaped at the chance to take a road trip as a welcome break from the miserable toil of their daily lives. Many nobles, bored with life in their dark, drafty castles, stepped up too. For a lot of Europeans, it would be a one-way ticket to the Holy Land.

On the opposing side were the Muslims. In their more sophisticated culture, bathing and bathhouses were part of life, and the Muslims were appalled by the filthy, matted, buggy Christian crusaders. Still, each side brought its germs along, and when Muslims and Christians met on the battlefields, both weapons and insects slaughtered people on both sides.

Of the original three hundred thousand crusaders who marched on the city of Jerusalem in 1099, only about twenty thousand remained alive two years later. The majority died of diseases like malaria, plague, dysentery, and scurvy.

Movie versions of the Crusades tend to be funnier—and far cleaner—than the real thing.

A STEPPE UP

Genghis Khan

THE MONGOL LEADER GENGHIS KHAN (1162–1227) and this fierce armies thundered across Asia in a bloody tide of slaughter that created a huge empire. It extended across China and Russia and into central Asia as far as Eastern Europe. The Mongols had incredible riding skills—they ate and slept on horseback, and they made skillful use of stirrups. A Mongol warrior could turn in the saddle and shoot an arrow three hundred yards at a full gallop. Their home turf was the vast grasslands of the steppe regions, where their horses could graze, and they traveled between summer and winter pasturelands. A lively trade route sprang up north of the Silk Road, in more northerly climates. In these colder places, burrowing rodents provided warmth and comfort to their fleas all through the winter. Possibly this is where the plague **bacillus** came from.

Sometime in the 1340s, disease broke out in central Asia. Infected fleas may have hopped from rodents onto Mongol horsemen, who carried the disease across Asia and Russia and the Middle East, and southeast to India and China.

TMI — TOO MUCH INFORMATION?

LIFESTYLES OF THE FIERCE AND RUTHLESS

MONGOL SOLDIERS WEREN'T picky eaters. If there was nothing else available, they drank horse blood or ate mice, rats, and lice. Their trousers were typically made of goatskin. On top they often wore silk shirts (which made it easier to pull an arrow out of a wound) and tunics that Mongol women sewed from pieced-together rat skins for warmth.

FEAR AND FEVER IN THE FOURTEENTH CENTURY

IN 1345, THE WORLD'S SECOND MAJOR plague pandemic struck. It began at Caffa, a port city on the Black Sea (now in modern-day Ukraine). A skirmish broke out between the army of a Tatar prince from Mongolia and a settlement of Italian traders from Genoa. The Genoans hid behind the fortified walls within the town, besieged by the Tatar soldiers. Before long, the Tatars began to sicken and die.

Alarmed by how rapidly his soldiers were dying, the Tatar prince decided to retreat. After the Tatars had gone, the Genoans hurried to their ships and headed for home. But they were already infected with plague. By the time they reached Italy, most of the merchants and sailors were dead or dying. Some ships never made it back at all but drifted off with everyone aboard dead.

It quickly dawned on the people of the Italian port cities that the Genoan ships were carrying disease into their midst, so they fired burning arrows at the ships to keep them from docking. That forced the ships to head to other ports, bringing their fleas and rats and disease with them. The plague spread rapidly across the rest of Europe.

IT'S RAINING MEN

AS A PARTING SHOT before they retreated, the Tatar soldiers catapulted a few dead bodies over the walls of the fortress where the Italian traders were hiding. The plague may have spread to the traders from fleas on these dead bodies.

PLAGUED

MANY HISTORIANS BELIEVE THAT ONE reason the fourteenth-century plague was so deadly is that at some point the bubonic form of the plague transformed to the even deadlier pneumonic plague—just as it may have done during the Justinian plague before it (see Plague box, page 31).

"[Plague victims could] eat lunch with their friends and dinner with their ancestors in paradise."

—**Giovanni Boccaccio (1313–1375)**

Many people fled the cities in panic, leaving their families and friends behind to fend for themselves. Dead bodies piled up and were collected by cart drivers foolish or desperate enough to take on the job. The bodies were thrown into huge plague pits.

Commerce, farming, construction of buildings, and basic day-to-day living came to a grinding halt; people focused only on surviving.

Wolves entered many half-abandoned cities and devoured the dead in the streets. Ghost ships drifted at sea. Dazed survivors wandered through abandoned castles or staggered through empty towns.

There was no shortage of theories as to what had brought on the plague. Some people blamed it on the position of the stars and planets.

Bruegel's *Triumph of Death*, circa 1562, is about the plague. Not a cheery picture.

Others blamed cats, dogs, gypsies, lepers, cripples, and, most notoriously of all, Jews. Rumors circulated that the Jews had poisoned the wells. Even though members of all these groups were dying of plague at the same rate as everyone else, there were widespread mob executions of innocent groups of people.

The last thing people suspected to be the cause were the fleas that inhabited their homes and bodies.

BUGGED

NO BACKSIES!

MANY PEOPLE BELIEVED that the plague was God's punishment for their wickedness. To atone for their sins, some tried to give all their money away to the Church. In one town in Germany, panicked members of a congregation stampeded to the local church with fistfuls of money in their hands, but the priests locked them out for fear of catching plague. So the mob simply threw their money over the locked gates of the church.

WHACK JOBS

ONE OF THE MOST OUTRAGEOUS EFFORTS to prevent plague was practiced by a group of people called the flagellants (FLAH-juh-lents). To "flagellate" means to whip (from the Latin word *flagellum*). The flagellants' idea of begging for God's forgiveness was to beat themselves bloody. They wandered from town to town, publicly whipping their own backs with iron-tipped lashes until the blood ran from the wounds. As they gained in popularity, the flagellants became more and more fanatic, and crowds by the thousands would come out to watch them—which allowed fleas to jump from person to person and caused the plague to spread even faster.

The flagellants seemed to have little interest in the organized Church. In some places they grew more popular than the pope. They also encouraged attacks against Jews. In 1349 the pope ordered them outlawed.

DOWNSIZING AND RESTRUCTURING

ALTHOUGH IT WOULD CONTINUE TO recur from time to time, the worst of the plague was over by 1350. In its aftermath, big changes swept through the structure of European society. The social order began to crumble.

Knights returning from the Crusades found their lands neglected, their castles looted. Peasants revolted, knowing that their labor was now more in demand because there were fewer people to do the work. The Church saw its power weakening, in part because many survivors' faith was shaken by the suffering they had seen.

This new way of thinking occurred all the way up the social ladder, from laborers to merchants to kings and queens. Many people turned away from the Church toward more here-and-now pursuits like creating art and seeking education and building up personal wealth.

EAST MEETS PEST

MEANWHILE, BEFORE THE PLAGUE STRUCK, the Byzantine Empire (see Constantinople, page 49) had grown into a bustling, prosperous "second Rome." And Baghdad (which today is in modern-day Iraq) had become one of the centers of the Islamic empire. In the seventh and eighth centuries, the Arabs had expanded their empire across North Africa and into the Iberian Peninsula (see Un-Moored, page 63). Huge strides were made by Arab scholars in the fields of mathematics, medicine, and astronomy. And Arabs introduced the world to sugar, rice, and coffee.

But the plague changed everything. The once-mighty Byzantine Empire was devastated by the plague in 1347 and shrank to just the city of Constantinople, which fell to the Turks in 1453. Farther to the east, China lost half its population, and the Mongol Empire toppled, giving rise to the Ming dynasty. The tiny flea took down mighty empires.

8

More Thinking but Still Stinking: The Renaissance

THE DUNG AND THE RESTLESS

AFTER A HUNDRED YEARS OR so, the worst of the plague had passed, and survivors could at last turn their minds away from its horrors. Great thinkers began to consider what it means to be human, to prize individual accomplishments, and to question the absolute power of the Church. The Renaissance dawned. Poets and philosophers and painters revisited the works of the ancient Greeks and Romans, and produced incredible masterpieces of their own.

There goes the neighborhood.

ENDLESS PATIENTS

DURING THE RENAISSANCE, MOST ORDINARY people still lived in filth and squalor, and many died young from disease. A great many children did not live to see their first birthday, and fewer still celebrated their fifth. Sanitation was awful, food was bad, and hardly anyone bathed. Bugs were everywhere—and doctors, who still knew very little about how diseases were transmitted, used appalling treatments that tended to speed up the deaths of their patients (see There Will Be Blood box, below).

THERE WILL BE BLOOD

FOR CENTURIES, DOCTORS BELIEVED that diseases were caused by body fluids being out of whack. Unfortunately for their patients, doctors often decided the problem with their patients was that their bodies needed to get rid of "bad" blood. Bleeding was a common treatment for fever, headaches, inflammation (swelling of various body parts), and pretty much every disease anyone came down with, including those transmitted by insects. The medical practitioner—usually

Shave? Haircut? Bleeding? One-stop shopping!

someone called a barber surgeon—opened a vein on the patient's arm with a knife. The dripping wound was held over a basin to catch the blood, often until the patient fainted from blood loss.

Blood-sucking leeches were another way to remove "corrupt" blood. Applying a ring of leeches around the head was thought to cure a headache, while putting fifty on the abdomen might cure obesity.

After being bled, patients were often purged as well, a process that involved drinking disgusting concoctions that made the person either vomit or have terrible diarrhea. No wonder so many patients died.

SEE? NOW DON'T YOU FEEL BETTER ALREADY?

AGE OF EXPLORATION AND EXPLOITATION

MANY BRAVE ADVENTURERS FELT A new restlessness to explore the world. And many kings and queens were eager to stake out new territories in faraway places. Because most Europeans considered themselves superior in every way to people who were not European, these kings and queens believed it was their divine right to conquer and rule over non-Europeans if they so chose. Mostly, though, the explorers and the kings and queens they reported to were after two things: gold and spices.

THE SPICES OF LIFE

THERE WERE NO REFRIGERATORS during the Renaissance. That meant that food went rotten quickly. Poor people were used to holding their noses and eating spoiled, smelly food. But wealthier people had slightly higher standards. Spices and salt were extremely useful for keeping food from spoiling and for repelling maggots and weevils and moths. The problem was, spices grew in only very faraway places, such as India, and were extremely expensive. Europeans desperately wanted to find a shortcut to India to avoid having to sail all the way around Africa. So they tried heading west. That's how they happened to bump into North America.

Salt: the center of everything

UN-MOORED

IN SPAIN, THE CHRISTIANS FOUGHT THE Moors (Muslims from North Africa and Spain) for control of the southern part of the peninsula (now made up of Spain and Portugal). Eventually the Christians won. By the late 1400s, the newly Catholic country of Spain rose from the ashes of the Muslim empire. Its rulers, Ferdinand and Isabella, were extremely intolerant of non-Christians (notably Muslims and Jews). During the long years of fighting between Moors and Christians, soldiers on both sides were felled by disease, including epidemics of a new and mysterious spotted fever, which was most likely typhus. In a 1489 battle with the Moors, the Spanish generals discovered that this strange disease had killed seventeen thousand Spanish soldiers, compared to the mere three thousand who had died from battle wounds.

The Spanish would shortly take their diseases with them across the Atlantic and introduce them to the New World.

NOW WE'RE GETTING SOMEWHERE—BUT WHERE?

AFTER SACKING THE MOORISH CITY of Grenada in 1492, King Ferdinand and Queen Isabella were now proud rulers of the whole Spanish peninsula. Seeking more ways to enrich their kingdom, they gazed out at the Atlantic and wondered if they could get to Asia quicker by sailing west, rather than having to go all the way around Africa to the east. They sent Christopher Columbus to find out.

You've probably heard that Christopher Columbus discovered America. This is not true. For starters, there were already people living there. But in those days Europeans considered a place unexplored until a European arrived at it.

Second, Columbus was not even the first European; others had been there before him. But the clincher is that Columbus never actually set foot in North America at all.

On the famous voyage of 1492, the *Niña*, *Pinta*, and *Santa Maria* bumped into a "new" continent, which Columbus declared was India. In fact, it turned out to be the Bahamas. He would make several more voyages west over the course of his lifetime, and he continued to insist for the rest of his life that he'd found India. He called the natives "Indians" and named the part of the Caribbean where he'd landed the "West Indies."

Although he was quite wrong about his geography, his voyages did make Europeans aware that there was a New World across the Atlantic Ocean.

You Don't SAY

"For the execution of the voyage to the Indies, I did not make use of intelligence, mathematics, or maps."

—Christopher Columbus

GERM WARFARE

FERDINAND AND ISABELLA BEGAN FUNDING more expeditions to the New World. The Spanish and Portuguese explorers called themselves "conquistadores" (conquerors), and they favored very silly hats. Their main interest was finding silver and gold.

On the upside, the voyages nearly quadrupled what Europeans knew of the globe. On the downside, when the Europeans encountered native populations, they enslaved, robbed, murdered, and conquered them. The first to arrive in large numbers in the New World during this Age of Exploration were the Spanish and Portuguese, followed later by the English and French.

How were so few Europeans able to conquer these huge populations of people? The Europeans had guns and horses, to be sure, but they were still vastly outnumbered. The main reason was that the Europeans were walking petri dishes. They infected the natives with their diseases, many of which were bug-borne.

Great ancient civilizations crumbled as New World people died in droves from European diseases—the Incas in South America, the Aztecs in Mexico, and the Mayas

A beads-for-disease diplomatic swap

in what is now Guatemala and Mexico. With no immunity to the Old World diseases, somewhere around 90 percent of the native people died. They had never before encountered tertian malaria (an especially deadly strain of the disease), yellow fever, dengue, smallpox, measles, diphtheria, typhoid, scarlet fever, or influenza, all introduced by Europeans and (later) enslaved Africans.

The European invaders remained reasonably healthy, because they encountered very few diseases that were new to them.

MOTLEY CRUISE

SHIP FOOD FOR SAILORS was famously dreadful. The water stored in barrels tasted vile. Food spoiled. The standard fare was biscuits made of flour and water. These biscuits were so hard they could break a tooth (assuming one had a tooth) and had to be soaked before eating. In humid climates the biscuits were quickly colonized by creepy-crawly weevils (the larval stage of certain beetles).

ARRRRGH!

AFTER FERDINAND AND ISABELLA kicked the last of the Moors out of Spain in the late 1400s, many of the Moors joined forces with the Barbary states—Tripoli, Tunis, and Algiers—all parts of the Ottoman Empire. The disgruntled Moors became pirates who preyed on Christian ships. Piracy in the southern Mediterranean became a huge problem from the sixteenth to the nineteenth centuries. The Europeans were outraged that the Barbary pirates often seized the gold that the Europeans had just stolen from people across the Atlantic.

Pay up. *Padre.*

"We Spaniards know a sickness of the heart that only gold can cure."

—Hernando Cortés

DEPLORABLE EXPLORERS

Hernando Cortés (1485–1547)

I N 1519 SPANISH ADVENTURER HERNANDO CORTÉS conquered the massive Aztec Empire with just a few hundred raggedy men and some microscopic, poisonous pathogens.

The Aztec leader, Montezuma II, controlled a vast empire that stretched from the Atlantic to the Pacific in what is now Mexico. Montezuma's big mistake was believing that Cortés was a god. An Aztec legend had predicted that according to their admittedly confusing calendar, this was the year that a fair and bearded sun god would be showing up to take back his land. Montezuma believed that Cortés was that god, and the Spaniards played along. It's hard to feel too sorry for Montezuma, who was despised by neighboring tribes. He was famous for approving mass human sacrifices of captured warriors and would sooner hand you your still-beating heart than shake your hand.

Be that as it may, Montezuma came to realize that Cortés was not a god at all, and that the Spaniards were simply interested in stealing his gold and silver. But it was too late by then; the Aztecs were already dying of mysterious and horrible diseases.

The previously unexposed native people died in shocking numbers. The Spaniards had immunity to the old-world diseases they'd brought along with them, and they hardly got sick at all. Before the Spaniards arrived, the Aztecs' capital city, Tenochtitlán, had had a population of three hundred thousand people. When Cortés marched into it with a few hundred soldiers in 1521, half of the city's inhabitants had already died of disease. Both sides thought that the diseases and suffering were signs of God's displeasure with the Aztec people. Stunned and grief stricken, the wretched survivors surrendered.

GLOBE TROTS

NOWADAYS, **IF A TOURIST** to modern Mexico suffers an attack of diarrhea, it is known as Montezuma's revenge.

Juan Ponce de León (1474–1521)

MEANWHILE, AROUND THE SAME TIME, a Spanish explorer and slave trader named Juan Ponce de León went in search of the Fountain of Youth (if certain accounts are to be believed). He'd recently helped Spain claim the West Indies and Meso-America (the land between North and South America, also known as Central America). León sailed north from Puerto Rico and landed in a new place, which he named *Florida* (Spanish for "flowery"). It became a Spanish territory in 1513.

Standing about four foot eleven, León was amazed to discover the natives there were over six feet tall. Surely this was the site of the Fountain! In fact, the place turned out to be quite the opposite—thanks to swarms of mosquitoes, it was an unhealthy, malarial swampland. In 1521, León tried to colonize the western coast of Florida, where the natives were a lot less friendly. He was wounded with a poisoned arrow and died later of the infection.

PONCE DE LEÓN DISCOVERS the FOUNTAIN of MOSQUITOES

DIG IN

SWARMS OF MOSQUITOES IN FLORIDA were so thick that early explorers dug themselves holes and slept on the beach covered in sand.

Francisco Pizarro (1478–1541?)

IN 1533, CORTÉS'S SECOND COUSIN, Francisco Pizarro, arrived at what is now Peru with an even smaller band of "conquerors." Only 168 Spaniards, along with a few African and Indian slaves, marched into the heart of the Incan Empire, intent on conquering ten million natives. By the time Pizarro and his men had huffed and puffed their way up through the Andes Mountains, they discovered that the Incas were already reeling from disease. Measles and smallpox had taken a terrible toll, followed by another mysterious and deadly fever that made people bleed from the nose and become delirious—possibly typhus.

Taking advantage of the natives' terrible condition, Pizarro captured the Inca leader Atahualpa (ah-tah-HUAL-pa). Atahualpa offered a huge ransom for his own release, which was worth the equivalent of millions of dollars in gold and silver. Pizarro accepted the ransom but treacherously executed Atahualpa anyway.

Hernando de Soto (1500–1542)

HERNANDO DE SOTO WAS ANOTHER conquistador with a keen interest in personal enrichment and a shocking disregard for human life. He had accompanied Pizarro on his expedition to conquer the Incas. In 1541, he traveled across what are now Florida, Alabama, Georgia, Arkansas, and Mississippi, massacring natives as he went. He eventually "discovered" the Mississippi River, even though Native Americans had been living in that area for centuries. He died of a tropical fever. Most signs point to malaria.

Giovanni da Verrazzano (1485–1528)

VERRAZZANO WAS NOT SPANISH, BUT Italian, and he was sent by the French king to find a western route to China. He never found the route but kept himself busy plundering riches from Spanish ships. He was supposedly the first European to see New York Harbor, and today the Narrows at the entrance to the bay is named after him, along with the bridge that spans it. (Oddly, the Verrazano Bridge and Narrows are spelled with one less *z*.)

WHAT A WAY TO GO

THE JOB OF AN EXPLORER has never been a healthy one. Here's how some of the explorers died:

Ferdinand Magellan: shot with arrows and (possibly) eaten by cannibals

Hernando Cortés: fever (possibly insect-borne) or dysentery

Juan Ponce de León: infection from a poisoned arrow wound

Francisco Pizarro: stabbed by guys who didn't like him

Hernando de Soto: malaria

Sir Francis Drake: yellow fever or malaria

Sir Walter Raleigh: ordered beheaded by Queen Elizabeth's successor, King James

Giovanni da Verrazzano: eaten by cannibals

Henry Hudson: set adrift in a small boat by his mutinous crew

9
Travel Troubles

WORKERS IN CHAINS

BY THE MID-1500S, THE SPANISH AND French had established huge plantations of sugarcane in Hispaniola (now Haiti and the Dominican Republic), Jamaica, Puerto Rico, and Cuba. But a problem arose. Where were they going to find people willing to work

in the steaming-hot, bug-ridden sugarcane fields? The Europeans certainly didn't consider doing the work themselves. And native people died too quickly from European diseases. So plantation owners decided to use slaves who were used to tropical places.

Farther to the north, on what is now the eastern coastline of the United States, English and French landowners were thinking along the same lines. They tried to use the labor of convicted prisoners, indentured servants, and various other Europeans who had been kicked out of their own countries for speaking out against their governments. But these workers also tended to die from disease. Where to find workers who didn't get sick so easily? The answer, they all concluded, was Africa.

European slavers shackled, enslaved, and shipped the first African slaves across the Atlantic Ocean to North America in the late sixteenth century. They came from the west coast of Africa, and the dreadful traffic of human cargo flourished during the seventeenth century. Enslaved Africans unwittingly introduced yet more diseases to the New World.

ANTS IN THEIR PLANTS

IN 1518, AFTER SPANISH SETTLERS HAD ESTABLISHED HUGE PLANTAIN, banana, and sugarcane plantations in Hispaniola, a plague of fire ants (*Solenopsis geminata*) swept across the island. People's homes were *teeming* with stinging ants. The fire ants were so numerous that people slept on their roofs or were driven off the island entirely. Whole plantations were wiped out "as though fire had fallen from the sky and scorched them," recorded a firsthand witness.

A world-renowned ant specialist, E. O. Wilson, does not believe the fire ants destroyed the crops. More likely, another, sap-sucking insect, which had probably hitched a ride from Africa along with the plantains and bananas, was doing the damage. The sap suckers were protected by the fire ants in exchange for the sweet honeydew they excreted. Without any natural predators, the sap suckers—and then the fire ants—multiplied.

House-swarming parties

POX BOX

YELLOW FEVER

YELLOW FEVER STARTS with a blinding headache and painful sensitivity to light, followed by a high fever. Sometimes the person feels better for a few days, only to experience the return of the fever. One bizarre symptom that sometimes afflicts the victim is nonstop hiccupping.

In serious cases, the virus attacks the liver, which causes the skin to turn bright yellow to deep gold (depending on the person's original skin tone) and the whites of the eyes canary yellow. The kidneys stop functioning, which poisons the body and causes the victim to bleed internally. The victim may then vomit black blood (see Dr. Black Vomit box, page 105). Death often follows. The yellow skin tone of victims earned the disease the nickname "yellow jack."

FORCED MIGRATION

ENSLAVED AFRICANS ENDURED HARROWING VOYAGES across the Atlantic. Although some Africans had resistance to smallpox (not bug-transmitted) and malaria (bug-transmitted), other diseases, most notably typhoid, typhus, scurvy, and dysentery, took a deadly toll on the suffering people packed into the filthy, cramped holds of the slave ships.

Yellow fever and tertian malaria most likely had not existed in the New World before the sixteenth century. Another tragic consequence of slavery is that the slave ships probably carried the mosquitoes' larvae in their water barrels and introduced these diseases to the New World. Although many Africans had some resistance to yellow fever, which had existed in Africa for centuries as a relatively mild childhood illness, New World natives had none. Once it showed up in the New World, yellow fever killed fast. Major yellow fever outbreaks struck British Barbados, Cuba, and Yucatan during the mid to late 1600s.

For more than three hundred years, tens of millions of Africans were sent to the New World against their will. Millions of them died of disease and mistreatment. But the ten million or so people who survived the voyage across the Atlantic Ocean and were able to endure the terrible working conditions on the plantations became extremely valuable to slave owners. As a result, the slave trade became more and more firmly established as part of the Caribbean economy (and later, that of the southern United States).

Meanwhile, the loss of tens of millions of people from the African continent crippled Africa's economic development for centuries.

BUZZ OFF!

CARIBBEAN PLANTATIONS WERE DEADLY PLACES to live and work. The cost of transporting slaves across the ocean was high. So why didn't the Europeans just conquer Africa and establish their plantations there? Parts of Africa were just as fertile as the Caribbean.

Certainly the Europeans weren't bothered by their consciences. As a matter of fact, they *tried* to conquer and colonize Africa, many times.

The mosquito protected Africa from European colonists. The tsetse fly helped too. Bug-borne diseases posed a problem in the Caribbean, but they were *much* worse in Africa, and they killed Europeans in high numbers. Malaria mowed down soldiers. Sleeping sickness killed their horses.

There were no roads in most of Africa, so the only way to travel inland from the coastlines was by river—and we know what was buzzing around *that* water. Sleeping sickness, yellow fever, and malaria kept Europeans confined to coastal areas. The west coast of Africa became known as the "dark continent" and also "the white man's grave."

DENGUE FEVER

DENGUE FEVER IS A VIRUS transmitted by the same species of mosquito that transmits yellow fever. It is known as breakbone fever because of the awful joint and bone pain the person experiences. Victims may suffer a high fever, severe headache, vomiting, and sometimes a rash. It usually lasts two to seven days, and victims tend to recover, though a second bout with it may be fatal.

BANTU POWER

THE BANTU PEOPLE OF WEST AFRICA had a powerful advantage over many other Africans. During the course of several thousand years of living with the mosquito that transmits malaria, they acquired some resistance to the disease. As a result, the Bantu were able to live in the interior parts of Africa, pushing other tribes to the outer areas of the continent. So it's likely that their resistance protected them at least somewhat from invasion by outsiders—including slave traders.

A Bantu tribesman posing in a nineteenth-century photography studio

POX BOX

MORE AWFUL TROPICAL AFFLICTIONS

YOU ALREADY KNOW ABOUT sleeping sickness, transmitted by the tsetse fly (see Sleeping Sickness box, page 30). But another disease that occurs in tropical places and is especially bad in parts of Africa is called **filariasis**, also known as **elephantiasis**. You can get it if a fly or mosquito bites an infected person and then bites you, infecting you with microscopic worms. The worms interfere with the body's ability to fight infection and drain fluids from the arms and legs. Some people experience no symptoms, but others suffer from grotesque swelling of certain parts of the body.

River blindness is caused by another microscopic worm, which can be transmitted by a black fly or mosquito. The larvae swim through a victim's skin and can destroy tissue in internal organs. They can also cause blindness if the parasite travels into the victim's eyes.

10

It's All Fun and Games until Someone Loses an Isle

THE REIGN OF SPAIN IS PLAINLY ON THE WANE

SPAIN EXPERIENCED SEVERE OUTBREAKS OF plague and typhus throughout the sixteenth and seventeenth centuries. One major epidemic of plague in northern Spain may have killed half a million people. This large drop in Spain's population may be a big reason that Spain declined as a world power. Meanwhile, the English were gaining ground in the New World.

The Spanish and English hadn't exactly seen eye to eye ever since the English king, Henry VIII, outraged Catholic Spain by divorcing his Spanish wife, Catherine of Aragon, in 1530, after she failed to produce a male heir. The Spanish were also growing increasingly peeved because English privateers (pirates who work for a king or queen) were stealing a great deal of the gold that the Spanish had stolen from the natives in the New World. By the time Henry's daughter, Queen Elizabeth I, was on the throne, in 1558, English privateers had become very skilled at plundering Spanish ships. And the most famous of all the English privateers was Sir Francis Drake.

Catherine, the first of Henry's six wives, pleading her case. He didn't listen.

THE STRUGGLE FOR THE STRIP: SIR FRANCIS DRAKE (1545–1596)

SIR FRANCIS DRAKE WAS A man who played many roles. He was the first Englishman to sail around the world. He may have introduced the potato to England from South America. He was an expert navigator and ruthless fighter. He was also a slave trader. Where opinions differ is whether he was a dashing adventurer loyal to his queen to the end (what the English thought) or a common pirate (what the Spanish thought).

In 1585, full-fledged war broke out between England and Spain. When England defeated the Spanish Armada in 1588, Drake was second in command. England became the most powerful nation in the world.

In 1595, Drake was back in the looting business. He and his fleet set sail again for the West Indies, determined to gain control over the Isthmus of Panama, which

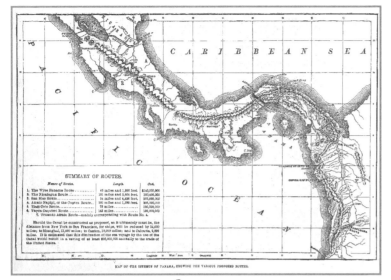

Panama

was still held by the Spanish. An isthmus is a narrow strip of land that connects two larger chunks of land—in this case, North America and South America. The Spanish had been using the isthmus to transport their loot back to Spain. Slaves had been forced to make the forty-mile trek on foot, from the Pacific side of the isthmus over to the Atlantic side, which was much quicker than having to sail around the southern tip of South America. Many of those African slaves carried the malarial and yellow fever parasites in their blood. The Central American mosquitoes that bit them also acquired African parasites. The Panamanian jungles, which had already been unhealthy, became notoriously deadly places.

But Drake was determined to seize the isthmus anyway, despite the dangers. In 1596, his ships moored off the bug-ridden western coast of present-day Panama. Soon his men began to sicken and die from what may have been malaria, typhus, yellow fever, or a combination of all of those. Drake himself caught a fever and died in delirium.

The English would continue to try to control that narrow strip of land separating the Atlantic and Pacific for the next 250 years. But they would never succeed. (See Zoning Out, page 120.)

THE BRITS BRANCH OUT

WITH SPAIN ON THE WANE, the English decided to take a crack at colonizing the New World. Sir Walter Raleigh was another privateer employed by Queen Elizabeth, who, like Sir Francis Drake, was masterful at plundering Spanish ships while wearing lace, high heels, and drop earrings. (Hey, it was the fashion.)

In 1587, Raleigh sent a group of 150 people to establish a colony on an island off the coast of present-day North Carolina. But when English ships returned to the place three years later, the colonists had all vanished. What happened to the "lost colony" remains a mystery to this day, although it seems likely to have been a combination of starvation, mosquitoes, and hostile natives.

The English settlers finally managed to start a colony in 1607 in Jamestown, Virginia. Half of the settlers did not survive the first winter. Starvation, typhoid, dysentery, and malaria probably killed many of them.

But the English continued sending more and more of their religious radicals to the New World. It seemed like a convenient way to get rid of them. Those who survived the diseases grew increasingly immune. Eventually, Jamestown began to prosper.

FOR GOD, NOT GOLD

UNLIKE THE PREVIOUS EXPLORERS, WHO came to the New World in search of gold, the colonists who arrived later came in search of religious freedom. (This difference would have been lost upon the natives, who were eventually forcibly relocated by both groups.) The Pilgrims sailed over on the *Mayflower* and founded Plymouth, Massachusetts, in 1620.

Ten years after the Pilgrims came the Puritans, another extreme faction of Protestantism. They settled in Salem, Massachusetts. Despite the colder climate, people who managed not to die of starvation and scurvy could at least look forward to a less buggy existence than that endured by the colonists farther to the south.

Before long, the Pilgrims and Puritans in the north enjoyed a population boom and higher life expectancy than the colonists living farther south in the malarial Chesapeake Bay.

By now, landowners in the southern colonies had established a prosperous slave trade to keep their cotton and tobacco plantations running. Charleston, South Carolina (then called Charlestown), had the largest slave market in the colonies and was also the sickliest place to live.

MAYFLOWER POWER

WHEN SOMEONE SAYS "PILGRIM," you probably conjure up an image of a person in a silly hat, somber black clothing, and buckle shoes. (In fact, the Pilgrims dressed much more colorfully than that.) Who were the Pilgrims?

The Pilgrims were religious separatists who got kicked out of England. They fled to Holland and, eventually, fearing for their safety to practice their religion, crammed onto the *Mayflower* to sail to the New World. There were 102 Pilgrims and 20 to 30 sailors aboard the *Mayflower*. The voyage took sixty-five days, and the ship was beset by storms, headwinds, and leaky decks. They arrived in Plymouth, Massachusetts, in November and were forced to spend the winter aboard the ship. By spring, half of them had died of cold and disease. And yet the colony would take hold. Eight American presidents were descended from the fifty-five survivors of the *Mayflower* voyage.

Seasick settlers

THE BARK IS BETTER THAN THE BITE

DURING THE 1600S, SOME SPANISH priests in Peru noticed that the local Incas possessed a miraculous medicine for fever and chills. They drank a bitter-tasting mixture made from the ground-up bark of a cinchona tree. The Spaniards took possession of the Incas' traditional medicine. They brought the bark back to malaria-ridden Europe, where people soon discovered it didn't just lower a person's fever, it seemed to prevent the person from getting malaria as well. Cinchona became wildly popular and worth more than its weight in gold. For hundreds of years this bark would be the only known treatment for malaria in the Western world.

But because it had been brought back to Europe by Spanish Catholics, many English people distrusted it. The seventeenth century was not known for religious toleration. In Protestant England, cinchona was scornfully referred to as "Jesuit bark." The gloomy, fiercely anti-Catholic English leader Oliver Cromwell refused to take the bark for his malaria and probably died of the disease.

THE TREE OF LIFE

CINCHONA BARK CONTAINS QUININE, a chemical compound with antimalarial properties. The bark was ground to a fine powder and mixed with a drink, usually wine. In 1820, a couple of chemists figured out how to extract the quinine from the bark, and thereafter quinine was sold in pill and powder form.

THE SPANISH ARE COMING! THE SPANISH ARE COMING!

IN 1655, A GROUP OF ENGLISH SOLDIERS landed in Cuba, intending to establish a colony there. They were startled to see a great many lights advancing toward them from the forest and assumed it was an army of Spaniards. So they hightailed it back to their ship and went on to settle Jamaica instead. The lights were not an advancing army. They were a species of click beetle, which resembles a firefly.

FLEAS AND DISEASE: THE BLACK DEATH RETURNS

BACK ACROSS THE ATLANTIC, ANOTHER epidemic of bubonic plague swept through crowded, filthy London in 1665.

People still had no idea what caused the plague. Many believed poisoned air was responsible. Others thought cats somehow triggered the epidemic, and in a stunning act of bad judgment, the mayor of London had all the cats destroyed. As you can imagine, the absence of cats, natural predators of rats, led to more rats and more fleas.

What Not to Wear during a Plague Epidemic: Victims' Clothes

DURING THE OUTBREAKS OF BUBONIC PLAGUE of the seventeenth century, it was widely believed that you could catch the plague by touching a victim's clothing. This idea wasn't far from the truth, as the plague was spread by the bite of a flea, and fleas did tend to jump off one person's clothing and onto another person. And because clothing was so valuable, it's highly likely that the clothes of dead plague victims found their way to the used-clothing markets.

In 1665, a tailor in a small village in Derbyshire received a box of clothing from London. Two weeks later, the tailor was

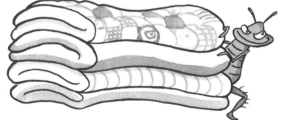

dead. The rector of the town decreed that no one should leave the village (for fear of infecting others). When the plague eventually ran its course, by October of the next year, fewer than 40 villagers remained alive, out of an original population of 350 people.

Rope Trick

IN HOMES WHERE ONE person caught the plague, the entire household would be sealed for forty days until the victim either recovered or died. (So it's likely many people died of starvation rather than plague.) A guard would be posted in front of the house to ensure no one escaped. Stories circulated of one family that carefully lowered a noose from an upper-story window and hanged the guard to escape.

OH, HONEY DON'T!

HONEYBEES ARE NOT NATIVE TO NORTH AMERICA. The first bees were brought over by colonists in 1622, where they quickly took hold and thrived.

Nowadays, the bee of choice is the Italian honeybee, *Apis mellifera ligustica*. But in 1952, some beekeepers in South America attempting to breed Italian honeybees with an African strain, *Apis mellifera scutellata*, accidentally released the African bees into the wild.

The upside of African bees is that they are more resistant to parasites and produce lots of honey. The downside is that they are much more aggressive and more likely to sting. This strain of bee has migrated northward into the United States and has interbred with the European bees. These so-called killer bees are widely feared by the public, thanks in part to scary Hollywood movies about swarms of killer bees. People do die from their stings, usually from a severe allergic reaction.

Africanized bees have been known to remain in wait for victims as long as twenty-four hours. They can chase people more than one-quarter of a mile.

If you are ever chased by a swarm of bees, do not jump into water. The bees will hang around until you come up for air. The best thing to do is to run away and seek the shelter of a car or house. Africanized bees are slow fliers, so you should be able to outrun them.

It's only a movie!

How Revolutionary!

BUGGING THE BRITS

THE AMERICAN REVOLUTION, AS YOU probably know, began when disgruntled colonists, fed up with Great Britain's micromanaging and unfair acts of taxation, wrote the Declaration of Independence, organized an army, and put George Washington in charge of it.

But as with most wars, it was the insects that helped decide the outcome.

England's war with the American colonies was just one of the problems the powerful British Empire faced. By 1779, it was also fighting the French and the Spanish and the Dutch and squabbling with the Russians. As a result, Britain had trouble drumming up enough men to fight against the colonists. To fill the ranks, the British government emptied out its jails and put convicted prisoners in British uniforms. It will come as no surprise to you by now that many of these prisoners, living in filth and squalor, had jail fever, otherwise known as typhus. So, many soldiers on the British side were sick before they even arrived on colonial soil. By the time they got off the boat, hundreds had died and thousands more were ill. Disease spread quickly.

Besides suiting up convicts, another tactic the British used to add to their ranks was to hire mercenaries—people paid to fight. These soldiers from foreign places brought foreign insects with them. (See Bug Thug box, page 88.)

Meanwhile, in the southern colonies, malaria and typhus were ravaging the British ranks. American and French soldiers got sick too, but many colonial Americans had acquired some resistance to malaria, and the British soldiers were more frequently exposed.

So General Washington had both the female mosquito and the body louse on his side. He also had quinine. In 1775, the Continental Congress budgeted $300 for quinine for General Washington and his troops. The British and their German/Hessian allies had less confidence in the healing powers of "the bark."

George Washington

YOU DON'T SAY

"Kill no vermin, as Fleas, lice, ticks, &c in the sight of Others, if you See any filth or thick Spittle, put your foot Dexteriously upon it; if it be upon the Cloths of your Companions, put it off privately, and if it be upon your own Cloths, return thanks to him who puts it off."

—George Washington, age fourteen

BUG THUG

THE **TINY HESSIAN FLY** is a major pest of wheat to this day. It probably arrived in North America around the time of the Revolutionary War. A British general, Viscount William Howe, commanded German mercenaries in the war against the Americans. The fly may have arrived in straw bedding that these Hessians brought over on ships.

PRESIDENTIAL BUGS

SOME **INSECT-RELATED ILLNESSES** suffered by American presidents:

GEORGE WASHINGTON (president 1789–1797) malaria

JAMES MONROE (president 1817–1825) malaria

ANDREW JACKSON (president 1829–1837) malaria

JAMES K. POLK (president 1845–1849) cholera

ZACHARY TAYLOR (president 1849–1850) yellow fever, malaria, dysentery, possibly cholera or typhus

ABRAHAM LINCOLN (president 1861–1865) malaria

ANDREW JOHNSON (president 1865–1869) typhoid

ULYSSES S. GRANT (president 1869–1877) malaria

JAMES GARFIELD (president 1881) malaria

GROVER CLEVELAND (president 1893–1897) possibly typhoid

THEODORE ROOSEVELT (president 1901–1909) malaria

WILLIAM HOWARD TAFT (president 1909–1913) typhoid, possibly dengue fever, dysentery

JOHN F. KENNEDY (president 1961–1963) malaria

FEVER IN PHILLY

I N THE BRAND-NEW UNITED STATES, DISEASES struck with depressing frequency. People were especially terrified of yellow fever, and no wonder. Think how scary it must have been to watch a person turn canary yellow, vomit black blood, and then die.

In Philadelphia, an epidemic of yellow fever broke out in 1793. The disease probably came from mosquitoes that had hatched in water barrels stored aboard the many ships that had fled the yellow fever epidemics in Haiti and the West Indies.

At that time Philadelphia was the nation's capital—George Washington, John Adams, Thomas Jefferson, and many other Founding Fathers lived there.

Of course, no one yet knew that mosquitoes transmitted the disease. They thought it was transferred by touch or by bad air. People fumigated letters they'd received from cities suffering yellow fever epidemics, by poking holes into them and steaming them with formaldehyde gas.

One of the Founding Fathers, Alexander Hamilton (1755–1804), actually contracted yellow fever. He and his wife left town and traveled to New York City but were denied permission to enter the city. They then traveled to Albany, where they had to stay under armed guard while all their belongings were burned and their servants were disinfected.

Dr. Benjamin Rush, a prominent doctor who had signed the Declaration of Independence, was the first to diagnose the Philadelphia outbreak (see Lewis and Clark, page 94). He believed yellow fever arose from bad-smelling miasmas, and his advice to everyone was to leave town. For those who got sick, his treatment was to purge and bleed his patients (bad idea—see There Will Be Blood box, page 62). Intentionally causing patients to bleed was an unfortunate tactic, as yellow fever itself causes internal bleeding, so he probably

Doctor Rush: Bleeder of the Pack

hastened many people's deaths. But in spite of his misguided efforts, Rush worked tirelessly to tend yellow fever victims long after most people, including President Washington, his cabinet, and most of Congress, had fled the city. The American government came to a grinding halt. (Rush himself came down with the disease but recovered.)

The epidemic finally subsided with the onset of colder weather in November, which killed the mosquitoes.

BEETLE MANIA

CERTAIN SPECIES OF BLISTER BEETLES produce a poisonous secretion called cantharidin. If swallowed, it can be deadly. If it touches a person's skin, it can cause blisters. Cantharidins were a popular medicine well into the nineteenth century. They were used to treat bladder problems, earache, fatigue, and a host of other ailments. When you read about doctors from days of yore using a "blister poultice" on their patients, you can be pretty sure these poultices were made from blister beetles.

President George Washington, who was suffering from a sore throat and respiratory infection, was led to an early grave by his well-meaning but misguided physicians. His treatment included swallowing a poisonous compound of mercury. They also bled out more than five pints (almost half) of his blood. And blister poultices made from cantharidin were slathered on his body.

12

Dastardly Diseases and Demented Dictators

HAPPENINGS IN HAITI

BACK IN 1697, THE FRENCH had founded a colony on the west side of the island of Hispaniola. The Spanish ruled the east side. (Today the island is divided into French-speaking Haiti and Spanish-speaking Dominican Republic.) Both the French and the Spanish established huge sugar plantations and forced African slaves to do all the work. Slaves were treated with unimaginable brutality in the hot, buggy climate. The huge majority were men; plantation owners didn't bother to bring many women over, as most workers died young and were swiftly replaced.

Slaves toiling in the sugar fields

A hundred years later, at least four-fifths of the population of the Haitian side of Hispaniola was comprised of black slaves, nearly all of whom toiled in the cane fields. In 1791, the slaves finally revolted against their French oppressors. France sent troops across the ocean to squash the rebellion. Over 150,000 slaves were killed, but as many as 50,000 French soldiers also died. The French soldiers died not from battle wounds but from yellow fever.

In 1794, with thoughts of liberty, equality, and fraternity still fresh in their minds from their own recent revolution, the French finally abolished slavery throughout the colonies and declared Haiti's independence.

There followed several years of unrest, but in 1801, a charismatic man by the name of Toussaint-Louverture (1743–1803) declared himself governor for life of Haiti—

Toussaint-Louverture

that's basically code for "dictator." This annoyed the French, and it particularly annoyed Napoleon, a short, power-hungry general who had recently risen to power in France and become *its* dictator. Napoleon did not like to see someone else declare himself dictator—especially as Napoleon wanted to regain control over Haiti, re-enslave all the inhabitants, and take control of the profitable sugar business. So he sent 33,000 troops over to end the rebellion. Within months, almost 90 percent of the French soldiers had died of yellow fever.

Yellow fever had less effect on the black Haitian troops, most of whom were somewhat resistant from their repeated exposure. Haitians tended to suffer only moderate symptoms and recovered in a few days, unlike the Europeans, who suffered severe symptoms, and died at a rapid rate.

Napoleon decided Haiti wasn't worth the bother and withdrew. Thanks in large part to the yellow fever mosquito, Haiti became independent in 1804, the first country in Latin America to do so.

This was Napoleon's first major run-in with killer bugs, but it would by no means be his last.

NAPOLEON VERSUS THE ARTHROPODS: LET'S MAKE A DEAL

DURING NAPOLEON'S REIGN, THE FRENCH owned a huge chunk of land in North America—what is now part of the southern and midwestern area of the United States and what was then known as the Louisiana Territory. After the fiasco in Haiti, Napoleon decided he could also do without that hot, buggy territory, which he had battled Spain to acquire. In 1803, he sold it to Thomas Jefferson for about four cents an acre in a deal known as the Louisiana Purchase. He probably laughed his way to *la banque*, thinking he'd gotten the better deal.

Napoleon's sale of this vast territory hugely affected America's future, and world history in general. Americans were now free to expand westward. And eventually the Americans would figure out how to rid their territory of malaria-carrying mosquitoes.

Napoleon Bonaparte

"Doctors will have more lives to answer for in the next world than even we generals."

—Napoleon Bonaparte

LEWIS AND CLARK: HEAVY METAL

I**N 1803, THOMAS JEFFERSON SENT AN** expedition, headed by Meriwether Lewis and William Clark, to explore the new territory he'd just bought from Napoleon. He wanted them to find a route across the Rocky Mountains to the Pacific Ocean, and to collect information on people, plants, and animals along the way.

At the time the expedition set off, people of European descent had no idea what lay west of the Mississippi, outside of a few trappers, and no one asked them. Most Americans lived within fifty miles of the East Coast. And in those days, many people believed in hippogriffs and dragons. *Anything* could be out there.

William Clark

Meriwether Lewis

Meriwether Lewis was Jefferson's personal secretary. William Clark was a mapmaker and pretty good with boats. But neither knew much about the wilderness. Before the expedition, Jefferson sent Lewis to Philadelphia for three months to study up on botany, zoology, and medicine.

Lewis consulted with Dr. Benjamin Rush (the same doctor who took charge during the Philadelphia yellow fever outbreak; see Fever in Philly, page 89). At Rush's advice, Lewis brought along fifty dozen of Dr. Rush's Bilious Pills (high-octane laxative pills, which the expedition members came to refer to as "Thunderclappers"). These huge pills, about the size of a modern-day round breath mint, were a combination of calomel (mostly mercury with a dash of chlorine) and jalap (hot stuff—jalapeño peppers contain it). They took these pills for any number of ailments, including constipation, sore throats, and malarial fevers. Once when Lewis was downed by fever he took a dozen of Rush's pills. He claimed they restored him to health.

Lewis spent one-third of his budget on cinchona powder, mosquito nets, and hog's lard (which they smeared over their skin to keep away mosquitoes).

It was a grueling journey. Guided by a pregnant Shoshone girl named Sacagawea (who stopped briefly to give birth and then proceeded to carry her infant on her back the rest of the way), the thirty-three members of the expedition nearly died of starvation, and everyone had malaria and dysentery from time to time. Lewis got shot in the butt and chased by a grizzly bear. But arguably the worst part of this challenging journey was the bugs.

Mosquitoes were so thick, people had to eat in the smoke of the campfire, and still they managed to swallow dozens of mosquitoes with their food. Gnats and ticks and biting flies added to the torment.

But they made it to the Pacific and back again. Only one person died, probably from a burst appendix.

"The Mosquitoes and Ticks are noumerous & bad."

—William Clark, June 16th, 1803

THE WHOLE WIDE WORLD

MEANWHILE, BACK IN FRANCE, NAPOLEON promoted himself to emperor in 1804 and got busy trying to take over more territories.

Undaunted by his losses in the New World, and having conquered Spain, Italy, Austria, and Prussia, Napoleon decided his next task en route to becoming Evil Mastermind of the World would be to grab control of India from the British. He knew the British had much better naval skills than the French did, so he didn't risk a sea battle. Instead, he decided to send his troops to India on foot. Have a look at this map. Country names and borders may have changed since 1812, but it's still a long walk from France to India.

One pesky problem was Russia, which would need to be conquered along the way. But Napoleon probably thought this would be a mere bump in the road.

In the summer of 1812, the French set out for Russia with over 500,000 troops. By the time they crossed into Poland, as many as one-fifth of them were dead or too sick from typhus and dysentery to continue. Food was scarce, and hygiene and sanitation were appalling. Napoleon's soldiers drank polluted water and slept in the open or inside filthy, bug-ridden peasants' dwellings.

When the French troops marched into Russia, the army was down to about 130,000 men, felled mostly by typhus. As the army arrived in Moscow on September 14, the French discovered that the retreating Russians had burned down the city and surrounding fields and destroyed most of the food stores before fleeing. Famine, typhus, and dysentery killed more and more French soldiers. When they straggled back in retreat, freezing, sick, and starving, as few as 10,000 remained.

The French retreat from Moscow was one of the worst military defeats in history. In 1813, Napoleon raised *another* half-million men to try again to take over eastern Europe. Half the army died of typhus.

In 1815, Napoleon was forced to step down. The British sent him into exile on a tiny island in the south Atlantic. But it had been typhus, not the British army, that put an end to Napoleon's dream of world domination.

Napoleon's former soldiers cheering for him. They were probably delirious with fever.

PESTS GO WEST

AS THE NINETEENTH CENTURY PROGRESSED, PEOPLE gradually began to understand that improving sanitation was a good bet for preventing disease. But they remained unaware that insects might be making them ill. The period of 1820 to 1860 was a sickly time in the young United States. Michigan was a huge malarial swamp. The average age of death in the city of Boston was only 21.4 years (due largely to disease caused by poor sanitation and overcrowding). During the 1849 gold rush, as people flocked west to California in a mad quest for bling, insects and the diseases they carried hitched a ride too.

The settlers had little trouble taking over California and Oregon from the local Indian tribes, who were a bit distracted by the struggle to survive European diseases, including malaria.

POX BOX

CHAGAS' DISEASE

NAMED FOR CARLOS CHAGAS, the Brazilian doctor who identified its protozoan (a kind of protist) in 1909, the disease is transmitted by the blood-sucking triatomine, otherwise known as a kissing bug. It climbs on your face while you're sleeping, bites you around the lips (or eyes), and poops on your face. The pathogens are in its poop; you become infected when you rub or scratch the bite, and the germs get rubbed into the bite. (Assassin bugs are related to kissing bugs—see Death by Bug box, page 100.)

Victims may develop a fever and swelling at the bite site, but the big problems often don't show up for fifteen or twenty years after being bitten. These include enlarged liver and spleen, dementia (mental problems), weakening of the heart, serious problems with the digestive tract, and sometimes death.

THE ORIGIN OF HEEBIE-JEEBIES

CHARLES DARWIN WROTE THE ***ORIGIN OF SPECIES,*** a book that changed the way people understand life and evolution. During his voyage as a naturalist on the ship the *Beagle* (1831–1836), he spent five years exploring many tropical places. He may also have contracted Chagas' disease.

In *The Voyage of the* Beagle, Darwin recorded an encounter with bloodsucking bugs while in South America. "At night I experienced an attack (for it deserves no less a name) of the *Benchuca*, a species of *Reduvius*, the great black bug of the Pampas. It is most disgusting to feel soft wingless insects, about an inch long, crawling over one's body. Before sucking they are quite thin but afterwards they become round and bloated with blood. . . ."

Although Darwin had been known for his healthy appetite and vigorous constitution, his health declined upon his return to England. For the rest of his life he suffered from stomach ailments, general weakness, and ultimately a fatal heart disease.

For years some people chalked up his symptoms to hypochondria (a mental condition where you think you're sick even if you don't have symptoms). It wasn't until well after his death that scientists finally identified the protist that caused the disease. Although we'll never know for sure, many scientists believe Darwin had Chagas' disease.

Charles Darwin

DEATH BY BUG

THERE ARE DIFFERENT SPECIES OF BUGS that belong to the family *Reduviidae*, which includes kissing and assassin bugs. Some are actually beneficial, preying on crop pests. The mouthparts of assassin bugs are pointy two-way straws. The bug injects a poison that turns its prey's insides to soup. It then sucks them dry.

Some species of assassin bugs prey on larger animals, like humans. The bite of certain species of this bug is more painful than the sting of a hornet (see Hey! Ouch! YEEEOWWWWW! box, page 36). Assassin bugs were used as torture instruments by a few deranged central Asian caliphs (rulers) in the nineteenth century. Prisoners were thrown into bug pits to die slowly and painfully.

What are some other cheery ways humans have used insects to kill one another? One nineteenth-century explorer in Africa reported that driver ants were used as a grisly method of executing condemned prisoners, who would be tied up close to the ants' nests.

In ancient Persia, condemned prisoners were tied to a canoe; doused with honey to attract bees, flies, and other biting insects; and set adrift in the hot sun to die a lingering death. We'll spare you the details.

13
The Nineteenth Century: Crawling toward a Cure

OF LICE AND MEN—THE IRISH POTATO FAMINE

YOU'VE PROBABLY HEARD ABOUT THE Irish potato famine, otherwise known as the Great Hunger. But you may not be aware of what a huge role bugs played in this tragic period of Irish history, when approximately three million people either died or fled the country.

Throughout human history, typhus has gone hand in hand with famine, drought, and war. It's been called famine fever for good reason. A starving person has a weakened immune system, which makes it easier to get sick with typhus.

The cause of the potato blight was not an insect but a fungus. The fungus struck Europe in 1845 and spread from place to place by the wind. The fungus thrived in warm,

Famine and fever

damp climates (such as Ireland's). It could turn a field of healthy potatoes to black, stinking mush in a single day.

That's what happened year after year between 1845 and 1851, which had unusually wet seasons. Although many European countries also suffered from the blight, Ireland was particularly hard-hit. It was already a very poor and overcrowded country, with more than nine million people. Many of them were farmers who relied on their single crop, potatoes, which they grew on tiny plots of land. Many Irish families lived almost entirely on potatoes. When the crop failed, they began to starve. People sold their clothes for food, then wandered in search of more food, naked or in rags. It was then that typhus—and other diseases, including typhoid, cholera, and dysentery— began to spread.

In 1846 the blight was worse than ever, followed by a harsh winter in 1846–1847. The weak, sick, wretched population huddled together for warmth in tumbledown shacks and ditches or staggered toward port cities and traveled by ship to England, Scotland, and America. They spread typhus everywhere they went. To add to the misery, in 1849 a deadly strain of cholera roared through, killing tens of thousands more in Ireland and elsewhere.

This happened at a time before governments felt a responsibility for the well-being of their poorer citizens. Ireland at the time was ruled by Britain, and the Irish (and people elsewhere) perceived British rulers as indifferent to their suffering and therefore slow to act. Eventually the British established workhouses for desperate Irish families, who were expected to work in exchange for miserable lodgings and meager food. The heavy labor and unsanitary, crowded conditions inside the workhouses resulted in the spread of yet more disease. Thousands of Irish people died of typhus in the bug-ridden workhouses.

Although the Great Hunger began with famine, ten times more people probably died of typhus, cholera, and dysentery.

Ireland's suffering as depicted by an American magazine of the time

A CRIMEAN SHAME

THE CRIMEA IS AN AREA of Ukraine, between Russia and Turkey. In March 1853, Russia invaded Turkey (then known as the Ottoman Empire). Britain and France grew concerned that the Russians were expanding their territory a bit too enthusiastically. So they sent soldiers to Turkey's aid. Eventually Sardinia joined their side as well.

Almost immediately, the body count from disease soared, amid dreadful sanitary conditions for wounded soldiers. Soldiers on both sides suffered from malaria, cholera, and typhus. And no wonder—the British hospital was built on top of a massive cesspool (a pit into which waste is deposited) and was a smelly and buggy place.

What made the Crimean War different from so many others? Florence Nightingale (1820–1910) appeared on the scene. Along with her team of volunteer nurses, Nightingale not only dramatically reduced death rates from diseases, but she also changed people's minds about nursing.

Back then, women from the "gentle classes" were discouraged from becoming nurses. It wasn't considered a ladylike job. Most nurses at the time were poorly trained and uneducated. Nightingale's wealthy family was shocked at her choice of such an unsuitable profession. But she went to the Crimea anyway and used her influential friends to publicize the appalling conditions in the British army hospital. Nightingale was finally allowed to clean up the place. Although no one at that time knew that lice were the source of typhus, her insistence on a clean, well-ventilated hospital meant fewer soldiers were bothered by lice, and deaths from typhus and other insect-borne diseases dropped. Before long, nursing became a legitimate profession.

Florence Nightingale

YOU DON'T SAY

Walt Whitman (1819–1892) was a famous American poet who served as a volunteer nurse during the American Civil War (1861–1865). He reportedly stated that war "is about nine hundred and ninety-nine parts diarrhea to one part glory."

Grubs in the Grub

THE CIVIL WAR WAS THE last major American conflict to be fought without people knowing how germs and bugs and microbes were related and how diseases were spread. Florence Nightingale's cleanliness standards hadn't yet become routine procedure. Basic sanitation was practically unheard of in the military camps. As a result, countless soldiers from both sides contracted malaria, dysentery, and diarrhea. The drinking water was filthy, and latrines were open trenches. Food was awful.

Union (Northern) soldiers were issued flour-and-water biscuits known as hardtack, and the biscuits were usually infested with bugs.

By this time, scientists had figured out how to make quinine from cinchona bark, and the pills were much easier to swallow than the bitter, powdered form of the bark. But supplies of

Civil War soldiers and their meager meal

quinine to both the North and South were frequently held up, and thousands of soldiers died of malaria.

About three out of five Union soldier deaths, and two out of three Confederate, were due to disease rather than battle wounds. The South fared worse because there were a lot more insects in the warmer southern climate, especially in the swampy low-lying areas of the southern Mississippi River. Mosquitoes, biting flies, sand flies, and gnats were a maddening problem for the soldiers.

DR. BLACK VOMIT

LUKE PRYOR BLACKBURN (1816–1887), a Confederate doctor from Kentucky, hit upon what he thought was an ingenious plan. He would start a pandemic of yellow fever in the North. On two occasions in 1864, he traveled to Bermuda, where a yellow fever epidemic was raging, and arranged to have trunks full of infected clothing and bedding from yellow fever patients shipped to major northern cities. He believed this method might introduce yellow fever into the North. Some of the clothing was also intended for President Lincoln himself.

His plan did not work. He did not know that mosquitoes, not dirty laundry, spread the disease.

Blackburn became known as "Dr. Black Vomit," which refers to one of the symptoms of yellow fever—victims often vomited what looked like coffee grounds but was actually blood from internal bleeding. Blackburn fled to Canada after the war to avoid prosecution. He later returned and became governor of Kentucky in 1879.

A PLAN THAT BACKFIRED

IN 1865, A MAN NAMED E. Leopold Trouvelot set out to try to breed a new kind of silkworm. He was trying to establish a silk industry in the United States. The experiment went horribly wrong.

He kept his moths under protective netting at his home in Medford, Massachusetts. A few years later, some of them escaped and were scattered by a high wind. Over the next twenty years, the population of moths exploded. We know them as gypsy moths.

Nowadays these destructive tree caterpillars are considered extreme pests. Gypsy moths have spread beyond New England toward many other parts of the country, as well as into southern Canada, and they devour the leaves from millions of acres of trees every year.

HOPPY DAYS

IN 1862, PRESIDENT LINCOLN SIGNED A new law to get people to move to the Great Plains as a strategy for keeping this new territory slave-free. (The Great Plains are the huge area of land west of the Mississippi and east of the Rocky Mountains.) The new law was called the Homestead Act, and it allowed anyone to claim 160 acres of government land after farming it for five years.

A great many people from the eastern United States, as well as newly arrived immigrants from Europe, leaped at the offer of free land where the soil was rich and fertile for farming.

But settlers discovered that the weather on the Great Plains was harsh, with brutal winters and hot summers. High winds gusted across the barren landscapes. It must have been a grim existence in the early days.

As if these hardships weren't enough, glittering clouds of locusts swarmed across

Abraham Lincoln

the American Midwest between 1874 and 1876, darkening the skies above the Great Plains and ranging from the Dakotas all the way down to Texas. The sound the locusts made was compared to the roaring of a huge waterfall. Not only were crops devoured in minutes, but so too was the wool from the bodies of live sheep and even, according to some reports, the clothes off peoples' backs. Trains couldn't move along the tracks because the insects made the rails too slippery. The locusts, or hoppers, as people called them, remained for a few days to a week and then left as they had come, on the wind.

Pioneers made soup with boiled locusts. Given that the locusts had probably devoured everything else that was edible, eating them was a sensible idea—locusts are high in protein, low in fat.

INSECT ASIDE

THE BUZZ ON LOCUSTS

THE SWARMING ROCKY MOUNTAIN LOCUST that caused such misery in nineteenth-century America appears to be extinct. But the desert locust, another swarming species, is still a huge problem in Africa and parts of Asia.

GANGING UP

LOCUSTS ARE GRASSHOPPERS THAT FLY in huge swarms. The ravenous swarms do tremendous damage to anything growing. When solitary grasshoppers join together and form a huge group, it is called a mass streamaway.

Locust swarms can cover four hundred square miles and can darken the sky for days. Although they don't carry disease, locusts are extremely unwelcome visitors, able to eat their body weight in food every day.

Scientists have been trying to figure out what causes a harmless, solitary green grasshopper to go into swarm mode, changing—Incredible Hulk–style—into a voracious, brown flying locust. Researchers have figured out that a chemical called serotonin may be the key. Just a few hours after grasshoppers were injected with the chemical, they changed physically, becoming stronger, darker, more mobile—and a lot more social with one another. In the wild, swarms usually form after a rainy period that is followed by a dry spell. The rains cause populations of grasshoppers to increase, and then the next drought causes them to cram into smaller areas to find ever-scarcer food. It seems that when the insects start rubbing up against one another on the ground, something triggers the serotonin levels in the insects' brains that signal them to morph, and the swarm flies off to find greener pastures.

A modern-day locust swarm in Madagascar

CRASH COURSE

INSECT ASIDE

SCIENTISTS HAVE BEEN STUDYING locusts to try to learn how they avoid crashing into one another when flying in huge swarms. They hope to develop a crash-avoidance technology for cars, based on locusts' navigational skills.

Locusts have a large neuron behind their eyes that releases bursts of energy whenever the insect is on a collision course with another insect (or predator). To study this energy release, scientists parked locusts in front of a Star Wars movie and monitored the activity in their brains whenever the locusts perceived an object (like, say, the *Millennium Falcon*) flying directly at them. The time period between the insects' releasing spikes of energy and their evasive action was about forty-five-hundredths of a second. Scientists hope that someday soon cars can be equipped with a similar technology.

14

The Nitty Gritty about the Itty Bitty: Germs Discovered at Last

WOULDJA LOOK AT THAT!

BY THE EARLY 1880S, PEOPLE FINALLY began to come around to the idea that many diseases were caused by germs—rather than by miasmas or evil spirits. It helped that microscopes improved a lot, so scientists could see the tiny wriggly stuff through the newly powerful lenses. The two pioneers of the **germ theory** of disease were Louis Pasteur (1822–1895) and Robert Koch (1843–1910).

Quite suddenly, science galloped forward with major discoveries relating to cause, prevention, and treatment of infectious diseases. A few people suggested that some of these diseases might be transmitted by insects, but no one listened to these people. The idea that insects could pass a disease from one human to another just seemed too bizarre to be true. That mystery would not be solved for several more decades.

Louis Pasteur

OH, RATS! PLAGUE RETURNS

THE WORLD'S THIRD MAJOR PLAGUE pandemic struck in the early part of the twentieth century, and it may have been the most deadly of all. It began in Asia in 1892, somewhere on the Himalayan border between China and India. By 1894, the disease had made its way to Hong Kong. In 1896, it devastated Bombay, India (now known as Mumbai). In 1899, it came to San Francisco.

The disease continued to appear and reappear around the globe over the next thirty years. The worst of the deaths occurred in India, China, and Indonesia. In India alone, over twelve million people died. And still no one knew it was spread by fleas—at least at first.

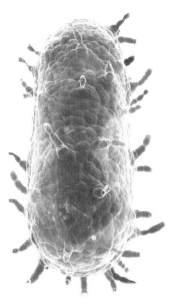

Bubonic plague bacterium

KITASATO AND YERSIN

In 1894, during the midst of this outbreak, two scientists discovered the bubonic plague bacillus almost simultaneously—Shibasaburo Kitasato (1853–1931) from Japan and Alexandre Yersin (1863–1943) from France. Although Kitasato and his team probably observed the bacillus six days before Yersin did, Yersin turned out to be the more careful scientist, and it was Yersin who suggested that rats might be a major factor in the transmission of the disease. Eventually, Yersin's more accurate results earned him the naming of the plague bacillus as *Yersinia pestis* in 1951. No, really. That's an honor.

Shibasaburo Kitasato

Alexandre Yersin

Flea Collarer

YERSIN WAS CLOSE WHEN HE suggested that rats might be the source of plague. But it took at least another decade for scientists to figure out that it was transmitted by the fleas *on* the rats.

OGATA AND SIMOND

Two scientists—Masanori Ogata in Japan (1896) and Paul-Louis Simond in France (1898)—  proposed the idea that fleas, rather than rats, were the transmitters of plague. But it wasn't until 1908, after several more scientists had re-created the earlier experiments, that scientists at last accepted the idea that the flea was the key.

Paul-Louis Simond

Even after people knew that plague was caused by a bacterium, and that it was passed from person to person by fleas, public health officials were no better equipped to prevent, treat, or cure the plague than had been their seventeenth-century predecessors. Their solution was to do what they'd been doing for centuries when plague struck: burn people's furniture, clothing, and houses and quarantine (isolate) victims.

It took fifty more years, and the discovery of antibiotics, before plague victims could be treated successfully. Nowadays plague is treatable if caught in time.

EEK! A FLEA!

INSECT ASIDE

COFFEE OR TEA?

DOCTORS HAVE LONG SUSPECTED that regularly drinking coffee might somehow protect a person from malaria. This theory may explain why the tea-drinking British have suffered more malaria than the coffee-drinking French did. It may also explain why Americans haven't been as bothered by the disease since they switched from tea to coffee as their preferred breakfast drink.

CATCHING THE FEVER: THE SPANISH-AMERICAN WAR

AS YOU KNOW, SPAIN RULED MUCH of Central America for centuries. But by the nineteenth century, its status as a world power had faded and its hold over Central America had weakened considerably. Cuba and Puerto Rico were the only Spanish territories left in the Western Hemisphere. The Spanish wanted to hang on to Cuba. But the Cubans felt differently. Three times the Cubans fought against Spain for their independence, starting in 1868. The last war of independence began in 1895, and in the last three months of that conflict, America jumped in to help Cuba fight against Spain. This became known as the Spanish-American War.

Why, you may ask, would this struggle between Cuba and Spain be any of America's business? Many Americans felt left out of the race to colonize other places. They thought the still-young United States had been so busy becoming an independent country, it had missed out on the chance to invade other places. These people thought America ought to establish colonies in other territories the way many European countries had done. And here was Cuba, practically in the backyard.

Americans in southern cities also wanted to clean up the notoriously unhealthy city of Havana, Cuba. A cleaner Havana might prevent diseases from migrating northward to American cities such as New Orleans and Memphis.

And finally, the story made for great drama. "Yellow journalism" is a term that came into use at this time. (The term is not related to yellow fever.) Joseph Pulitzer was the owner of the *New York World*, and William Randolph Hearst was the owner of the *New York Journal*, and they were fierce rivals. Each paper ran articles about the conflict that were full of exaggerations and downright false news. The papers' goal was to sell lots of newspapers.

An editorial cartoon from 1898, depicting Joseph Pulitzer (left) and William Randolph Hearst (right) and their struggle to use the Spanish American War to their advantage

When an American battleship called the Maine exploded while sitting in the Havana harbor in February 1898, killing 260 American servicemen, the yellow press had a field day. The sensationalist newspapers convinced many Americans that the Maine had been sunk by a Spanish submarine. Headlines screamed, "REMEMBER THE MAINE, TO HELL WITH SPAIN!" (The explosion was most likely caused by an oil leak.)

On April 25, 1898, Congress declared war on Spain. This delighted the jingoists (people who wanted to go to war), but the catch was, Americans then had to send troops to Cuba, and Cuba was a buggy, unhealthy place.

American soldiers had no sooner arrived than they began to get sick. Fewer than four hundred American soldiers were killed in combat during the war. But more than two thousand died of yellow fever.

On December 10, 1898, Spain and the United States signed a peace treaty. The treaty established the independence of Cuba. Spain gave Puerto Rico and Guam to the United States, as well as the opportunity to purchase the Philippines from the Spanish for $20 million. They also threw in Hawaii.

Meanwhile, the United States had thousands of sick soldiers to deal with. In yet another shameful example of mistreatment of the country's black Americans, the US Secretary of War ordered a regiment of African American soldiers to care for the sick. Possibly he believed them to be immune to tropical diseases, but he was wrong. Lacking the antibodies that their ancestors had acquired during a childhood in Africa, the American-born blacks died as easily as Europeans did. As many as one-third of those troops died of yellow fever or malaria.

KEEP YOUR GIN UP, MATE

IN THE NINETEENTH CENTURY, the British Empire controlled India. British occupiers in India already knew that quinine was indispensable for preventing malaria. They figured out how to improve the taste of the bitter medicine by mixing it with soda water and sugar. They called it tonic water. They mixed it with gin and added a bit of lime to help stave off scurvy. The gin and tonic soon became the go-to drink of the British Empire. By 1850, the British government was importing nine tons of quinine to India every year.

British soldiers taking their daily dose of quinine

BARKING UP THE RIGHT TREE

The bark is stronger than the (mosquito) bite.

OVER THE YEARS, MANY EUROPEANS had tried to steal the seeds of the cinchona tree from Peru. Peru was the only place in the world that grew the tree, and Peruvians had no interest in letting go of its world control over quinine. People who smuggled the seeds out were dismayed to discover that the seeds were too delicate to withstand the long voyages across the Atlantic. In 1862, an Englishman named Charles Ledger finally managed to steal and successfully cultivate some cinchona seedlings. Ledger tried to sell his treasure to the English government. But for whatever reason, the English government wasn't interested. So Ledger convinced the Dutch government of his seedlings' value. Holland established large cinchona plantations on the island of Java, their colony in Indonesia. The trees were not easy to grow, and it took at least ten years before they began producing bark with enough antimalarial compound to be worthwhile. But before long, the overharvested Peruvian trees died out, and the Dutch plantations became the only source of quinine in the world.

THE BRITISH INVASION

IT WAS ONLY WITH HEAVY DOSES of quinine that the British Empire finally succeeded in conquering the Asante Empire on the Gold Coast of Africa (modern-day Ghana) in the 1870s.

ANOTHER WONDER DRUG

CHINESE SCIENTISTS IN THE 1960S stumbled across an ancient Chinese medical journal that mentioned a plant that could cure malaria. They discovered that a shrub called Artemisia contains a substance possibly more effective than quinine. But the Chinese kept the drug, called artemisinin (are-TEM-is-in-in), a military secret for decades, and even after the knowledge was released to the rest of the world, it was not readily accepted in the West.

Eventually, most nations, including the United States and Britain, realized the power of this new drug, and artemisinin compounds have become widely adopted as safe and rapidly effective. Although recently, some malarial parasites are showing troubling signs of resistance to the artemisinin.

ALPHONSE LAVERAN AND RONALD ROSS

In 1884, a French army surgeon named Alphonse Laveran became the first person to see the malaria parasite under a microscope. He suspected that mosquitoes played a role in the disease, but he had no proof. The scientific community was skeptical. Everyone still thought the disease arose from bad-smelling mists in swampy places. But Ronald Ross (1857–1932), a Scottish army major stationed in India, decided to test the mosquito theory. By the late 1890s, after dissecting a lot of mosquitoes and successfully injecting the parasite into birds, he proved that the *Anopheles* mosquito was, in fact, the vector. (An Italian scientist named Giovanni Battista Grassi [1854–1925] came up with a similar discovery at around the same time, by infecting a human volunteer via the bite of an infected mosquito.) In 1902, Ross was awarded the second-ever Nobel Prize in medicine.

Ronald Ross

Alphonse Laveran

DOG TAG

THE RUSSIAN WRITER Anton Chekhov (1860–1904) named his dog Quinine.

BUZZ BUSTERS

AFTER THE SPANISH-AMERICAN WAR WAS over, the American army sent fifty thousand uneasy soldiers to Cuba to restore order. Many of them fell ill and died from yellow fever. Scientists still had no idea how the disease was spread. Most doctors thought it was spread by direct contact with a person or by touching infected clothing or blankets.

In 1900, the army sent a team of research scientists to Cuba to study the cause and spread of yellow fever. The team was led by Major Walter Reed. By now, the notion that a disease could be transmitted by a bug wasn't considered outlandish; Reed and his colleagues were

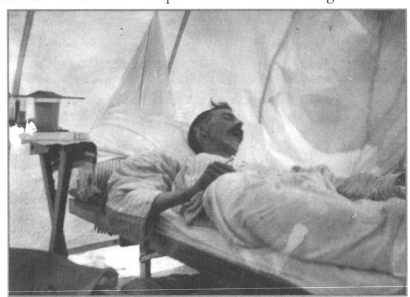

A yellow-fever patient in Cuba

well aware that three years before, Ronald Ross had proven that mosquitoes carried malaria. They set out to see if yellow fever might be transmitted the same way.

Going Viral

The Reed Dream Team, clockwise from top left: Reed, Aristedes Agramonte, James Carroll, and Jesse Lazear.

Died

Infected

REED'S TEAM OFFERED volunteers $100 in gold to participate in yellow fever experiments, with another $100 promised if the volunteer contracted yellow fever. Some of the volunteers were American soldiers; others were Cuban natives. If using human volunteers for such a dangerous experiment seems shocking to you, remember that, back then, it was quite common for doctors to perform experiments on volunteers or on themselves. In fact, two of the four doctors on Reed's team contracted yellow fever by allowing themselves to be bitten by mosquitoes. One of the team members died.

In those days of widespread prejudice, native people were generally considered plentiful and expendable and therefore good candidates for experimentation. As for the American soldiers who volunteered, it's very likely many of them figured they were going to get yellow fever anyway, so why not get it over with in a controlled setting with medical teams standing by—and get paid for it?

The researchers set up two camps. In one cabin, seven army volunteers put on the unwashed pajamas of dead soldiers and slept in victims' soiled sheets to see if they could contract the disease. The cabin was heavily screened to prevent mosquitoes from entering. The idea was to see if you could catch the disease by rubbing up against germy stuff. Although it must have been hot, smelly, and extremely unpleasant in the cabin, no one fell ill with yellow fever.

In the other cabin, thirteen Cuban volunteers were given clean sheets and clothing but mosquitoes were released into their living space. Eleven of the volunteers fell ill. This borderline-unethical but effective experiment clinched it: mosquitoes were the transmitters.

WALTER REED

Walter Reed and his team eventually proved that mosquitoes were the vectors of yellow fever. The result was a massive campaign to eliminate mosquito breeding grounds, provide people with protective screens, and spray a lot of pesticides. Cases of yellow fever in Cuba plummeted.

ZONING OUT

FOR CENTURIES, AS YOU'LL REMEMBER, European traders had been looking for a way to sail between the Atlantic and the Pacific without having to travel all the way around the southern tip of South America, (see Sir Francis Drake, page 78). In 1520, Portuguese explorer Ferdinand Magellan had found a strait (a narrow channel connecting two larger bodies of water—in this case, the Atlantic and Pacific). The Strait of Magellan made the trip a good deal safer weather-wise, but it was so close to the southern tip of South America that it didn't lop off much time in a voyage. A much more promising place to carve out a passage was at the Isthmus of Panama (at the time part of Colombia), where there was a narrow swath of land and which was much farther north (see map, page 79).

The French felt confident they could do it. How hard could it be to dig a forty-mile canal? After all, just ten years before, in 1869, they'd dug the hundred-mile-long Suez Canal in Egypt. That had considerably shortened the trip between Europe and Asia (it was no longer necessary to sail all the way around the southern tip of Africa).

So the French government launched an ambitious canal-building project. But it was a disaster. Workers dropped dead in droves from malaria and yellow fever. Their living conditions were primitive, unsanitary, and mosquito ridden. With a complete lack of concern for the working man that was typical of the era,

the architects of the project decided it was cheaper to replace dead workers than to improve working conditions or to try to restore the health of those who had fallen ill. But after eight hot, buggy, rain-drenched years, the French gave up. Over twenty-two thousand workers had died, and the canal remained unbuilt.

PAUL GAUGUIN, COMPANY MAN

THE FRENCH PAINTER PAUL GAUGUIN (1848–1903) was among the many French workers who came to Panama to work on the canal project. Gauguin hoped to work as a clerk and perhaps earn enough money to buy some land, live off tropical fruit, and paint. But the wretched working conditions he encountered at the Panama Canal site were much worse than he'd expected, and he left after two weeks.

I'm outta here.

Roosevelt (center, white suit) discussing the canal project with workers in Panama

Making the Connection

PRESIDENT THEODORE ROOSEVELT WAS NOT a man to be daunted by much of anything. He decided he would have a go at building the canal and bought the rights to the project for the United States in 1903. But Roosevelt had the good sense to pay attention to the findings of the Reed team of doctors. His plan included the same antimosquito measures in

Panama that had been used by Reed's team in Cuba, and he hired a doctor named William Gorgas to implement them.

The American plan worked. Malaria and yellow fever deaths dropped. The canal was completed in 1914.

WILLIAM GORGAS

President Theodore Roosevelt's hired medical enforcer, Dr. William Gorgas, was a tall, charming army colonel. (The nurses called him "Dr. Gorgeous.") Gorgas had worked for Walter Reed in Havana when Reed was establishing that the mosquito was the vector of yellow fever.

To eliminate mosquito breeding grounds, Gorgas's troops drained swamps and sprayed wet areas with pesticides. They poured oil into open drinking water receptacles, which coated the surface of the water and prevented mosquitoes from laying eggs. They installed screens on the windows of the workers' living quarters and even hired people (for ten cents an hour) to stay inside the living quarters to hunt down and swat mosquitoes.

Unfortunately the antimosquito campaign did not extend to all of the canal builders. Those with darker skin were assumed (incorrectly) to be naturally immune and were barred from the screened and fumigated cottages. It was an extremely prejudiced time.

Dr. William Gorgas overseeing the canal construction

Take Two Brandies and Call Me in the Morning

EVEN THOUGH THEY now knew yellow fever and malaria were transmitted by mosquitoes, people still had a hard time protecting themselves from being bitten. Bug spray didn't exist. To ward off mosquitoes, doctors advised people–including children–as they always had: drink a shot of whisky or brandy and puff on a cigar. It wasn't until 1937 that scientists developed a yellow fever vaccine.

VECTOR DETECTORS

CHARLES NICOLLE

In 1909, scientist Charles Nicolle (1866–1936) finally proved that the louse was the vector of typhus. He had noticed that typhus patients transmitted the disease to their families, to doctors who visited them, and to hospital laundry staff, but that once admitted to the hospital, the patients stopped contaminating people. Because all patients were washed and given clean clothes upon being admitted to the hospital, he quickly suspected the louse. After experimenting with laboratory animals, he proved the connection.

Knowing about the louse connection changed the way battles were fought during World War I (which began five years later, in 1914). It became routine procedure for soldiers to pass through delousing stations, going both to and from the front. This simple practice made it possible for millions of soldiers to huddle together in closely packed trenches without dying of typhus, which had been the fate of millions of soldiers in countless prior wars.

Charles Nicolle

15

Twentieth-Century Pox

INFECTIOUS INSECTS IN THE TWENTIETH CENTURY

THE FIRST DECADES OF THE twentieth century were a grim time in Europe. First, World War I began. Then disease struck. Lots of disease.

The war started in 1914 when a Serbian man assassinated the Austrian Empire's leader, Archduke Ferdinand. Austria declared war on Serbia. To avoid getting caught in the crossfire, Serbian civilians streamed out of the cities and into the countryside, where there was little food and shelter. The weakened, hungry refugees began to die of typhus, and before long the disease swept through the rest of Eastern Europe. The typhus epidemic reached a horrific peak in Russia between 1917 and 1923, where as many as thirty million people, already starving from food shortages and droughts, became infected. Three million Russians died. These disaster statistics

The CLEANEST fighter in the World—
the British Tommy

The clean, chivalrous fighting instincts of our gallant soldiers reflect the ideals of our business life. The same characteristics which stamp the British Tommy as the *CLEANEST FIGHTER IN THE WORLD* have won equal repute for British Goods.

SUNLIGHT SOAP is typically British. It is acknowledged by experts to represent the highest standard of Soap Quality and Efficiency. Tommy welcomes it in the trenches just as you welcome it at home.

£1,000 GUARANTEE OF PURITY ON EVERY BAR.

The name Lever on Soap is a Guarantee of Purity and Excellence.

LEVER BROTHERS LIMITED, PORT SUNLIGHT.

are hard for modern readers to comprehend. To add to the misery, 1918 was also the year of the worldwide flu pandemic (a deadly strain of bird flu, which killed more than fifty million people). The mind boggles at all that human suffering.

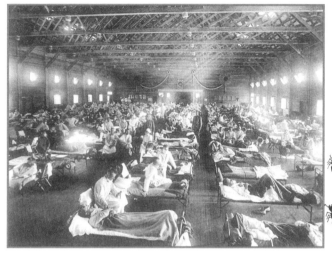
Spanish flu victims at an emergency military hospital

A LOUSY CHOICE

TYPHUS KILLED SO MANY millions of people during the 1917 Bolshevik Revolution that Lenin (1870–1924), the Bolshevik leader, remarked, "Either socialism will defeat the louse, or the louse will defeat socialism."

BUG THUG: BOLL WEEVIL

TO LOOK AT A BOLL WEEVIL, you'd never guess it's one of the worst of the crop crunchers. Fuzzy and brown, with a long snout, the boll weevil is a funny-looking bug. But the sight of it in a field causes even the toughest farmers to tremble. The weevil feeds on the boll, or pod, that contains the cotton fiber. It caused catastrophic damage in the southern part of the United States during the first part of the twentieth century.

EVIL WEEVIL

THE BOLL WEEVIL FIRST ARRIVED in the southern United States sometime in the 1890s. It probably came from Mexico, across the Rio Grande. Immediately, a war began between cotton farmers and this dreaded cotton parasite.

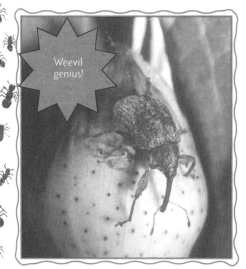

Weevil genius!

The weevil won the battle, if not the war. Over the next several decades, the insect spread across the southern United States until every cotton-growing state was infested. The boll weevil reshaped American society and American agriculture. Landowners went bankrupt. Sharecroppers left home and traveled north to find work. Between 1910 and 1930, the black populations of northern cities such as New York, Chicago, Detroit, and Cleveland increased by as much as 40 percent. Many whites moved to the suburbs, but because of widespread prejudice, black people were less free to settle where they wished. So black ghettos formed in larger cities. The crop devastation the boll weevil caused contributed to the mass migrations. Between 1915 and 1975, as many as six million African Americans left the South. The boll weevil helped usher in the Great Depression.

Meanwhile, farmers who stuck it out and stayed on their farms changed the way they farmed. Where before their only crop had been cotton, they began growing other crops as well, like peanuts, sweet potatoes, and soybeans. Luckily, the weevil wasn't interested in chomping its way through these crops.

An ongoing battle with the boll weevil continues to this day. Southern growers have learned to vary what they grow, to spray their crops by air, and to lure beetles into traps that contain chemical versions of boll weevil scent. It's helped a lot, but as we know, bugs tend to evolve faster than technology does.

SWAT TEAMS

IN 1941, THE JAPANESE BOMBED PEARL HARBOR and the United States entered World War II. US military leaders wanted American soldiers to have a warm, year-round place to train that had a climate similar to the tropical South Pacific (where many battles would be fought). But they quickly realized that something would have to be done about malaria, which was still a big problem in the southern United States.

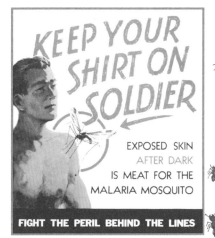

A malaria control office was built, with headquarters in Atlanta, Georgia. It was close to the Okefenokee Swamp, a major malaria-mosquito breeding ground. Armies of malaria-control workers fanned out across the southern United States from Florida to California, as well as Puerto Rico and the Virgin Islands, and sprayed areas where a mosquito might breed, using DDT (a pesticide; see The DDT Debate box, page 132), Paris green (a type of arsenic; see Going Green. Not. box, page 130), and diesel oil.

The campaign was a huge success. Malaria was eliminated in the United States. After the war, the malaria office was transformed into the Centers for Disease Control and Prevention, which is still in operation today.

QUININE CRISIS

REMEMBER HOW THE DUTCH HAD become the world's sole producer of quinine? (See Barking up the Right Tree, page 116.) They made a hefty profit selling their quinine to the rest of the world. But during World War II, the Japanese seized control of much of

Malaria patient, the South Pacific, 1943

Southeast Asia, including the Dutch-controlled island of Java. Their goal in taking over the cinchona plantations was to cut off the sole source of quinine to the Americans and other allied forces. Without quinine, the Japanese reasoned, the Americans would be reluctant to engage in battle in the South Pacific, where malaria was a huge problem.

The Japanese strategy worked. With all the world's supply of quinine in enemy hands, half a million or more American servicemen fighting in the South Pacific did contract malaria.

American scientists scrambled to develop a synthetic substitute for quinine. They did. For at least the next twenty-five years, chloroquine worked well. Heavily dousing people with DDT also helped. (See next chapter.)

16

The Craze about Sprays

LET US SPRAY

PEOPLE HAVE BEEN USING INSECTICIDES to battle pesky insects since ancient times. Pyrethrin is a common one that has been used for centuries. It's made from powdered chrysanthemum petals.

WHAT'S THE DIFFERENCE?

AN *INSECTICIDE* is a pesticide that kills insects. A pesticide is a more general term for a chemical that prevents, repels, or destroys various kinds of pests, including rodents, fungi, unwanted plants, or even bacteria and viruses—in addition to insects.

The earliest chemical pesticides were extremely toxic. Paris green, for example, is a powder made with a compound of arsenic. Although it's very good at killing insects, arsenic has also been a favorite murder weapon for many centuries. Two other early kinds of chemical pesticide were lead arsenate and hydrogen cyanide, both just as ominous as they sound. You don't have to be a chemistry major to figure out these were not good for the environment, let alone humans and other animals.

During World War II, many drug companies were widely praised for their success at controlling mosquitoes and lice, which prevented epidemics of many diseases. In 1943, for instance, a typhus epidemic in Sicily was avoided thanks to a required delousing of all civilians. Three million people, both civilians and soldiers, were dusted with DDT and other insecticides. "DDT" stands for "dichlorodiphenyltrichloroethane" (which is why it's just called DDT). It was hailed as a miracle chemical because it was inexpensive, effective, and not water soluble, so it didn't have to be reapplied after rains. The *New York Times* described this magical new potion as "deadly to insects" and "harmless to man." The Swiss chemist who discovered its use as an insecticide, Paul Muller, was awarded a Nobel Prize in 1948.

OH, BE-HIVE!

IN 1944, as part of the US military's impressive malaria-control campaign in the South Pacific, scientists invented something new: a five-pound canister that could spray insecticide through a nozzle in a fine mist. After the war, the canister was reformulated into a product bought by women with beehive hairdos: the aerosol can of hair spray.

GOING GREEN. NOT.

PARIS GREEN WAS MADE from a toxic arsenic compound that was used not only as an insecticide and an animal poison but also as a paint pigment. Some medical historians believe that the Paris green paint color so beloved by Impressionist painters may have worsened Vincent van Gogh's mental problems—he's the painter who cut off his own ear—as well as Claude Monet's failing eyesight. What's certain is that arsenical greens in wallpaper, fabric, and food poisoned a great many people over the course of the nineteenth century.

Ear today, gone tomorrow

INSECT ASIDE

SHOO FLY, DON'T BOTHER ME

"FLY WORRY" CAN BE A REAL PROBLEM for cows, horses, chickens, and other farm animals. Being bothered by too many flies can cause severe stress to the animals, causing them to produce less milk, lose weight, or lay fewer eggs.

PEST PROBLEMS CROP UP

AFTER WORLD WAR II ENDED, chemical pesticides were seen as the answer to everyone's insect troubles. But in the late 1950s, people in the northeastern part of the United States noticed something disturbing: robins were dropping dead. People found dead robins everywhere. It came to light that DDT had been sprayed on elm trees in an

effort to kill a bark beetle that was transmitting a fungus that caused Dutch elm disease. The DDT had been ingested by earthworms, which had been eaten by the robins. The dead robins were examined and found to have high concentrations of DDT in their brains.

At around the same time, US Department of Agriculture

(USDA) officials decided to try to get rid of the fire ants that were becoming a huge problem in the South. The bites could be quite painful to humans, and the ants destroyed plants and damaged cables and farm equipment. So the USDA began spraying DDT. After three million acres were sprayed, birds and small animals began to die. The USDA officials denied that the DDT was the reason for the animals' deaths and kept spraying.

Close encounters

A writer named Rachel Carson wrote a book about the chemical pesticides problem. She challenged the USDA's practices and claimed that it had never tested the sprays to see how dangerous they were to humans or wildlife. Besides which, Carson said, their random spraying hadn't gotten rid of the fire ants. Her book, *Silent Spring*, was published in 1962, and it created a huge controversy. Because DDT had been so successful at preventing typhus and malaria during World War II, many people accused Carson of being un-American.

But Carson's book was an instant bestseller. It sparked a modern environmental movement, which would eventually lead to the creation of the Environmental Protection Agency, the passage of the Clean Air and Clean Water Acts, and the banning of a long list of pesticides (including DDT).

And, the fire ants won the battle. Today they are found from Florida to California.

Rachel Carson

THE DDT DEBATE

HERE'S THE PROBLEM with DDT: it has saved a great many lives, but it has also caused serious environmental problems.

DDT and its related insecticides are not biodegradable. That means they don't break down quickly and may remain in the soil for years and years.

And when an animal, such as a worm, eats DDT, traces of the chemical remain in the animal's fat. If a larger animal, such as a bird, eats the contaminated smaller animal, the larger animal then stores the DDT in its body. So the higher up the food chain you get, the more and more concentrated the chemical becomes inside animals' bodies. Top predators in the food chain may eat or drink so much toxic stuff that they have problems reproducing, or, worse, the toxin kills them.

Another problem with DDT and so many other pesticides is that bugs have developed resistance. In other words, the pesticides no longer work on the pests, just the host.

In 1955, the World Health Organization began an intensive campaign to get rid of malaria in sixty countries by spraying DDT inside the homes of people in malaria-infested areas. At first, the campaign was a huge success. The number of malaria-transmitting mosquitoes was greatly reduced or eliminated in many countries. But thirty years later, the malaria mosquito had returned to fifty-eight of the sixty countries. A very few mosquitoes had been able to survive by developing immunity to DDT and similar pesticides. These were the sole parents of many new generations of hardy survivor mosquitoes.

SMOTHERING HEIGHTS

HERE'S A FACT THAT SHOULD alarm you: many of the nerve poisons developed during World War II as weapons against human enemies were reformulated after the war, in lower doses, to kill insects. The use of nerve poisons as weapons has since been banned by the United Nations, and they are classified as weapons of mass destruction.

So it's logical to wonder if the insecticides in use today may be harmful to living things that come in contact with them.

Exposure to organophosphate insecticides is nearly impossible to avoid in our society. (The "organo-" prefix shouldn't suggest that they're natural or good for you. It just means they contain carbon.) You can be exposed by breathing them in, consuming them, or even by just touching them. A study done in 2001 by the Centers for Disease Control and Prevention found traces of these organophosphates in 90 percent of the people they tested. Symptoms of pesticide poisoning range from headaches, depression, memory loss, and concentration problems to serious respiratory failure and death.

These insecticides are hard to avoid. Take lice shampoos, for example. Some of them contain the active ingredient lindane, which has very dangerous side effects. But if you or someone in your family has ever had head lice, you know that it is difficult to remain rational about long-term health consequences when all you want to do is get rid of those horrid little bugs in your hair.

A more recent class of pesticides seems more promising, biodegradable, and less toxic. Pheromones (basically, synthetic bug perfumes that smell good to other bugs) can control bugs by trapping them and disrupting their mating patterns. Pheromone traps can also help keep track of pest populations and movements. But even these pesticides are proving to be less and less effective as bugs develop resistance.

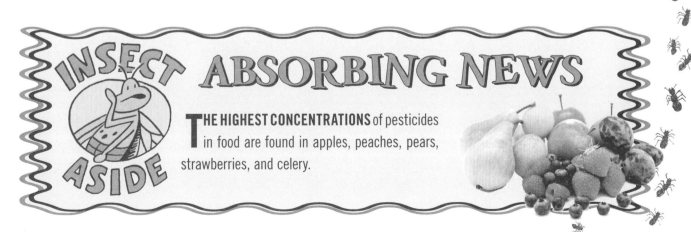

INSECT ASIDE

ABSORBING NEWS

THE HIGHEST CONCENTRATIONS of pesticides in food are found in apples, peaches, pears, strawberries, and celery.

BATTLE OF THE BEETLES

THE POTATO BEETLE may or may not have been used as a weapon during World War II. The Germans accused the Allies of planning to drop thousands of Colorado potato beetles on German potato fields; the Allies denied they had such a plan. It's no wonder the Germans feared for their potato dumplings; both the adults and the larvae of this pest are extremely destructive to potatoes and other plants.

Destructo-bug

SPARROW CHANGE

IN 1958, CHAIRMAN MAO Zedong of China introduced his "Four Pests" hygiene campaign, meant to eliminate rats, flies, mosquitoes . . . and sparrows. He ordered the killing of sparrows because he believed they ate grain seeds and prevented farmers' crops from growing.

Mao's officials mobilized people in cities and in the countryside. Everyone was urged to bang on drums and clash pots and pans to frighten the sparrows and keep them airborne until the birds dropped dead from exhaustion. Nests were destroyed, eggs broken, baby birds killed. The plan worked all too well.

By 1960, sparrows—and a number of other bird species—were driven to near extinction in China.

The delicate balance of nature was upended, with tragic results. Crop-eating insects were able to thrive, unopposed. In particular, swarms of locusts—a favorite food of sparrows—stripped bare the fields and crops, and millions of Chinese people died of starvation. Later Mao removed sparrows from the list.

17
Now What?

GLOBAL SWARMING

MALARIA, THAT ANCIENT DISEASE, WAS on the decline in many countries and was thought to be on the verge of disappearing forever. But in some countries, it has come back again. Mosquitoes have developed resistance to pesticides, and the deadliest malaria parasite has shown it is resistant to chloroquine, once the go-to drug for treatment. (Because of its troubling side effects, doctors rarely prescribe quinine anymore.) Malaria kills between one and two million people a year, and most of them are young children.

LESSER OF TWO WEEVILS: THE MULTIPRONGED APPROACH TO DEALING WITH INSECT PESTS

SO WHAT'S THE BEST WAY TO combat the insects that have acquired an immunity to pesticides? Is there a way to coexist with insects and still keep them from infecting us with diseases and devouring our fruits and vegetables?

Nowadays, scientists and entomologists tend to favor a combination approach to fighting insect pests and insect-transmitted diseases: pharmaceutical (controlling with chemicals), mechanical (often involving educating people as to how to avoid contact with the bad bugs), and biological (siccing a natural predator on the pest). In other words, the best way to battle bugs is limited spraying combined with smart farming practices combined with simple-but-effective pest control. It's known as **integrated pest management**.

How does this multipronged approach work?

Crops weren't the only things they sprayed back in the 1940s.

Prong One: Pharmaceutical

SOMETIMES, SPRAYING A LITTLE BIT is not as terrible as it sounds. But if you grow only one crop, you're asking for trouble (see Evil Weevil, page 126). Big industrial farms that specialize in one crop can help feed people more cheaply, but they also attract insect pests that specialize in eating that one crop, with no natural predators to keep them in check. So farmers have to do more and more spraying.

Take potatoes, for example. You know how vulnerable they are to insects and other diseases (see Of Lice and Men, page 101, and Battle of the Beetles, page 134). On huge industrial farms, the powerful pesticides they spray are absorbed deeply into the potato. The potatoes have to be stored for six months after they're harvested to allow the pesticides to leach out until the potatoes are considered safe for people to eat.

On smaller farms where a variety of plants are grown, pests may spoil one crop but can be completely uninterested in another. It's an argument in favor of small, local farms. Sometimes just a minimum of spraying can be very effective. Rotating crops is another good way to confuse insect pests.

The pharmaceutical approach includes treatment of bug-borne illnesses as well. There are still many medicines that make a huge difference in treating certain diseases. River blindness is now on the decline thanks to an inexpensive drug called ivermectin, which kills the baby worms inside an infected person's body. Although the adult worms aren't killed, at least the drug relieves the worst symptoms. And if it's taken for ten years (because the worms can live that long), the adult worms eventually die of old age, and the victim can be completely cured. There's evidence that the drug can also work against elephantiasis, (see More Awful Tropical Afflictions box, page 76). People are also given information about how to avoid reinfection.

Prong Two: Mechanical

SIMPLE MECHANICAL METHODS ARE A good way to help keep insects from transmitting diseases to humans. Take guinea worm, for instance (see Guinea Worm box, page 138). The World Health Organization has focused on teaching each household in affected areas to filter water that contains water fleas that carry the guinea worm larvae.

A simple solution is to use a T-shirt to filter the water, and to teach infected people to stay away from water when the worms emerge, so the worms can't re-enter the water and complete their life cycle. The result has been a dramatic drop in the number of cases of the disease.

Other low-tech solutions include giving people netting to protect themselves from insect bites when sleeping.

One way to combat Chagas' disease (see box, page 98) is by improving housing. Kissing bugs like to nest in thatched or palm-leaf roofs, which are common in poor areas. Helping people install sturdier roofs can reduce contact between bugs and humans.

Nets are a form of mechanical protection.

Mechanical controls can be as simple as raising or lowering temperatures. At many grain-processing mills, the temperature is raised for several hours at a time to kill weevils and other stored-food insects.

You can practice mechanical controls too. Rather than throwing smelly (and toxic) mothballs into your closet, put your sweater in the freezer for a day or two before you put it away for the summer, to kill any eggs laid by clothes moths.

POX BOX

GUINEA WORM

GUINEA WORM DISEASE, also known as dracunculiasis, is a dreaded disease that can be transmitted by drinking infested water that contains water fleas infected with a parasitical worm. Once inside the victim's body, the worm can grow to be up to a yard (meter) long. When the female worm is ready to release her larvae, she pokes out through a person's skin, usually in the lower leg. It's a slow, painful exit. The only way to get rid of the worm is to slowly wind it onto a stick over the course of several weeks until it has fully emerged. Because the exiting worm causes itching and pain, victims tend to plunge their leg into the nearest body of water for relief, allowing the larvae to be released into the water, which other people then drink. Symptoms of the disease include low energy, and stunted mental development in children.

Prong Three: Biological

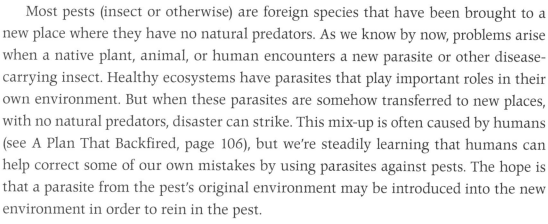

REMEMBER THE OLD LADY WHO swallowed a cat to catch the bird to catch the spider to catch the fly she swallowed? That's an example of biological control.

Scientists are always on the lookout for natural enemies of insect pests. The thinking is, even though insects may evolve and develop a resistance to certain pesticides, the predators that prey on these insects can evolve as well, keeping nature in wobbly balance.

Most pests (insect or otherwise) are foreign species that have been brought to a new place where they have no natural predators. As we know by now, problems arise when a native plant, animal, or human encounters a new parasite or other disease-carrying insect. Healthy ecosystems have parasites that play important roles in their own environment. But when these parasites are somehow transferred to new places, with no natural predators, disaster can strike. This mix-up is often caused by humans (see A Plan That Backfired, page 106), but we're steadily learning that humans can help correct some of our own mistakes by using parasites against pests. The hope is that a parasite from the pest's original environment may be introduced into the new environment in order to rein in the pest.

Here's an example of biological control: A team of scientists has been working on controlling the disease leishmaniasis (see Leishmaniasis box, page 140). They're planting certain types of vegetation that are poisonous to sand flies, which might kill the parasite in the fly's gut and help prevent the spread of the disease to humans.

And biological controls may help reduce malaria as well. Bacteria, plants, fish, and even ducks that feed on mosquitoes or mosquito larvae can help control mosquito populations.

HEY JOE — DOES THIS TASTE FUNNY TO YOU?

POX BOX

LEISHMANIASIS

LEISHMANIASIS (leesh-muh-NAHY-uh-sis) is a disease transmitted by a sand fly and is a major killer in parts of the world. Sand flies aren't good fliers and tend to move from one host to another in short, bouncy flights. Victims may experience skin sores; awful mouth and nose ulcers; and liver, spleen, or bone marrow infection.

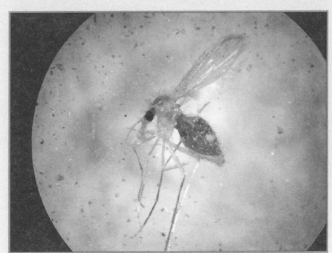

WINNING THE WORM WAR

THANKS TO A MASSIVELY successful prevention campaign led by former president Jimmy Carter, guinea worm disease will most likely be eradicated worldwide within the next few years.

SPACED OUT?

COCKROACHES DEPEND ON HUMANS for their food supply. They have followed the human trail of crumbs everywhere humans have ever lived. A cockroach was even spotted scurrying around on the *Apollo 12* spacecraft.

THAT'S SIX SMALL STEPS FOR A BUG!

PARASITES TO THE RESCUE

ONE EXAMPLE OF BIOLOGICAL CONTROLS may have saved a huge number of people in Africa from starvation.

The cassava plant has been an important food source to people in the southern part of Africa ever since Portuguese explorers brought it over from South America in the sixteenth century. It's also known as yucca and manioc. (And they make tapioca from it.)

Millions of Africans depend on cassava for 70 percent of their daily energy intake. The plant grows three feet high. Both its broad green leaves and its starchy roots are nutritious and edible, although you have to cook them; they're poisonous if you eat them raw. It can grow in rugged terrain, and it even withstands locust attacks.

Cassava plants in the field

In 1973, the plants began to shrivel up and die.

The culprit? An insect called the cassava mealybug. This was a major disaster, not just for one growing season but for many. To grow cassava, you need to plant new fields with cuttings of existing plants, so farmers lost crops year after year. Public health officials scrambled to figure out what to do.

A Swiss entomologist named Hans Herren studied where the bugs came from. He discovered that they were related to a cotton mealybug that lived in Central America (which is where cassava was originally cultivated). In 1980, he traveled to Central America and found a natural predator of the mealybug. It was a species of parasitic wasp that lays its eggs in mealybug larvae. This tiny wasp was smaller than the head of a pin, and it was very particular about what it preyed on—specifically, mealybugs.

Parasitic wasps have a pretty gruesome way of making a living. The female wasp lands on a living caterpillar and lays her eggs on its skin. The eggs hatch into larvae, which burrow into the hapless caterpillar and then, over time, proceed to eat their way out of their living host. In fact, the heartless practices of parasitic wasps horrified even Charles Darwin himself. Darwin wrote, "I cannot persuade myself that a beneficent and omnipotent God would have designedly created parasitic wasps with the express intention of their feeding within the living bodies of Caterpillars."

Mealybugs make meals for ants too.

Not a pretty picture—especially for the caterpillar

Herren and his fellow scientists were able to appreciate the wasp for its useful qualities. Working together with scientists in South America and Trinidad, they acquired a shipment of parasitic wasps from their native Central America, drugged them to make them sleepy, and then dropped canisters full of them from airplanes into the African fields full of diseased cassava plants. Within three months, the mealybug population plummeted.

More wasps were imported and raised in Nigeria and released into the wild. (They did not prey upon people, luckily.) The parasitic wasps spread across Nigeria, Kenya, and Mozambique, chomping their way through cassava-killing mealybugs until the cassava crops recovered by about 80 percent. Today mealybugs and wasps live in a natural balance. You wonder if knowing this story might have made Darwin change his mind.

TOO MUCH INFORMATION? TMI

THE UNDEAD

A CERTAIN SPECIES of parasitic wasp injects venom directly into a cockroach's brain that turns it into a zombie cockroach, still alive but unable to fight back. The wasp then pulls the zombie roach into its underground lair and lays an egg in its abdomen. The larva later hatches and begins to eat away at the inside of the roach. This takes about a week, during which the roach remains alive, sort of. It almost makes you feel sorry for a cockroach. (See Nice House, Nobody Home, pages 21–22, and Headless Horror box, page 144.)

WHAT COLOR IS YOUR PARASITE?

SINCE WE KNOW IT'S IMPOSSIBLE to get rid of parasites completely, maybe we can at least make them change. Some scientists believe we can force parasites to evolve into less harmful organisms by "taming" them. For example, public health workers give people screens and bed nets to keep malarial mosquitoes from biting (mechanical controls). With fewer people falling ill, it becomes harder for the malaria parasite to move from one host to another. If the parasite can't easily find a new host, it will be less likely to kill its host and may be forced to evolve into a gentler version of its former, deadlier self.

TOO MUCH INFORMATION? TMI

HEADLESS HORROR

TO COMBAT FIRE ANTS, Texas agricultural officials released a natural enemy known as a South American phorid fly (but it's not the same species of phorid fly that attacks honeybees; see Nice House, Nobody Home, pages 21–22). The fly injects its egg into the ant's head with a needle-like jab. The developing fly larva eats its way out of the ant, causing the ant to wander around like a zombie for about two weeks until its head falls off.

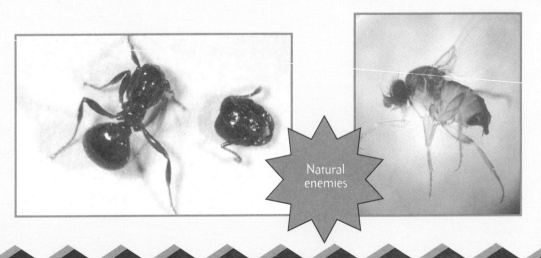

Natural enemies

INVASION OF THE BODY SNATCHERS

ANOTHER PARASITE, known as a hairworm, manages to brainwash grasshoppers by pumping them with a cocktail of chemicals that makes them jump into water and drown. The hairworms live inside grasshoppers' bodies. When the worms are ready to breed in water, they somehow sabotage their host's central nervous system and trigger the grasshopper's death leap into water so that the worms can emerge from the drowned grasshopper and complete their life cycle.

THE WORMS CRAWL IN, THE GERMS STAY OUT

HOOKWORMS, AND OTHER WORMS THAT live in a person's intestines, are a big problem in many poverty-stricken parts of the world. They can be spread from one person to another in different ways, including by way of insects. After they enter a person's body, the worms set up shop in the intestinal tract and mature into adults. They may live in a person's intestine for years, siphoning off blood.

As late as the mid-twentieth century, worms used to be a big problem in the southern United States and throughout much of Europe, but thanks to improved sanitation and the use of antibiotics, they're largely a thing of the past in these places.

Around thirty years ago, a few parasitologists—scientists who study parasites—traveled to places where parasitic worms are still a big problem. Then they made a startling discovery: people infected with intestinal worms appeared not to suffer as much from certain illnesses like hay fever, asthma, allergies, Crohn's disease, colitis, and a number of other diseases of the immune system.

These scientists proposed a controversial theory: perhaps

A Florida boy with hookworm disease, 1935

NOW WHAT?

our bodies don't "like" living worm-free. After all, people have lived with intestinal worms since caveman days. Maybe the worms somehow helped our immune systems fight off more serious diseases, and now that the worms are no longer in our bodies, our immune systems are going wacko, overreacting to the smallest environmental irritants and attacking our own bodies.

To test this theory, scientists conducted studies in which they deliberately infected people with intestinal worms. (In some studies scientists swallowed the worm eggs themselves. In others, they used volunteers desperate for relief from colitis and Crohn's that had not responded to the usual medicines.)

Here's what happened: within a couple of weeks of ingesting the eggs, which hatched into worms, most of the people who'd been suffering from these terrible illnesses became symptom-free.

No one is saying it's good to have worms. Hookworms kill thousands of people a year, usually in the poorest parts of the world. Most people with severe cases of intestinal worms develop anemia. Children suffer from stunted growth and malnourishment, and because their worms suppress their immune systems, they may be more likely to come down with other diseases.

But scientists are trying to figure out exactly how the worms influence the immune system to help the body resist those other environmental problems. They're hoping to use that knowledge to develop a vaccine that offers us similar protection, without the worms.

TOO MUCH INFORMATION? TMI

SHELF AWARENESS

YOU CAN STILL FIND TOILETS in countries around the world that are designed with a shallow shelf at the front of the bowl. This "lay and display" toilet design allows a person to examine his poop before flushing it away—a convenient way for a person to check the severity of his worm infestation. Sometimes there's a stick nearby, in case one wants to, well, give things a prod.

INSECT ASIDE

TERMITE TOWER

AN ARCHITECT HAS DESIGNED a building in Zimbabwe modeled on a termite mound. Termites build giant mounds and carefully regulate the temperatures inside by constantly opening and closing bug-built heating and cooling vents. Architect Mick Pearce and his team of engineers built a concrete building with a similar temperature-controlling system. Outside air is drawn in and either warmed or cooled by the building's structure. The building uses 90 percent less energy than a conventional building of its size.

Bug-built

Man-made

MORE MOSQUITO MISERIES

P X **B X** **POX BOX**

WEST NILE VIRUS was first identified in Uganda in 1937. Transmitted by mosquitoes, the virus probably arrived in the United States sometime in 1999 by way of airplane. You can be infected with the virus but not have symptoms. About 20 percent of people with the virus become sick. Symptoms may include high fever, disorientation, tremors, coma, paralysis, and sometimes death.

Encephalitis (en-sef-uh-LY-tis) is another virus transmitted by mosquitoes. It can range from mild to life threatening. Symptoms may include headache, confusion, fever, weakness, dizziness, seizures, and paralysis. Severe symptoms may include delirium, coma, and death.

WHAT'S A KID TO DO?
WHAT YOU CAN DO TO STAY HEALTHY

WE CAN—AND MUST—live in a world alongside insects. You can practice a few habits that will keep your own body healthy. Then work on educating your family, your school, and your community.

Here are a few things you can do right now:

- Don't buy perfect, blemish-free fruits and vegetables. They were probably treated with pesticides in order to look that good.

- If possible, start a garden of your own or join a local food cooperative or encourage your family to buy their fruits and vegetables at a farmer's market. That's a good way to minimize the amount of pesticides you're exposed to and supports smaller, local farms.

- Try to avoid eating fast food. A lot of the food that is grown for big chain restaurants comes from huge industrial farms that use a lot of pesticides and that grow single crops. Plus, admit it: the food may taste good, but doesn't it make you feel gross after you eat it?

- Alert your family to the fact that many household products are pesticides, including ant traps, bug sprays, flea medicines, cleaning disinfectants, products that kill mold and mildew, some lawn-care products, and some swimming pool

chemicals. It's practically impossible to avoid these products altogether, but try to limit your exposure to these things as much as you can, and try to educate your family about using the least-toxic products possible. Better yet, make them read this book.

• Understand that insects are part of the world and there's no way to make them go away. Remember that most of them won't hurt you, and a lot of them help. The key is to learn to coexist. And some insects are extremely cool.

• Don't panic about the possibility of an epidemic disease striking anytime soon. It's unlikely to happen, and most historically terrible diseases are now treatable. Scientists are making progress, learning how insect-borne parasites attack cells. But pay attention in science class and consider pursuing an advanced degree in the field of public health or epidemiology or entomology or parasitology. You may grow up to become a scientist who saves a lot of lives.

TERMS ABOUT GERMS, AND OTHER WORDS TO KNOW

arthropod: An invertebrate (animal with no backbone) that at some point in its life has an external skeleton, segmented body, and jointed legs. All insects are arthropods, but so are spiders, mites, centipedes, shrimp, and crayfish, which are not insects. Arthropods make up over 90 percent of the animal kingdom.

bacillus: A type of bacteria with a rodlike shape.

bacteria (singular is *bacterium*)**:** The smallest of all living things, these single-celled organisms are found almost everywhere. Most are harmless, but some—called pathogens—cause diseases. And certain insects transmit these harmful bacteria to humans. Serious insect-borne bacterial diseases include typhoid, bubonic plague, and typhus.

Colony Collapse Disorder: The abrupt disappearance of honeybee colonies.

endemic: A disease that regularly occurs in a population, over generations, and so people may experience less-severe symptoms. Chicken pox is an endemic disease; it used to kill people, but nowadays it's usually a fairly minor childhood disease.

epidemic: An outbreak of disease that infects a large group of people.

germ theory: A theory of disease that emerged in the latter part of the nineteenth century that states that microbes, or germs, cause disease, rather than the disease being spontaneously generated. Pioneers of germ theory included Louis Pasteur and Robert Koch. The theory was controversial in its day but is now widely accepted.

immunity: Resistance to a disease; the ability of a body's immune system to protect it from getting infected by a pathogen.

integrated pest management: The use of a variety of pest control methods that are designed to protect public health and the environment.

microbe: A tiny organism that can be seen only under a microscope. We all carry a huge number of microbes in our bodies, in our mouths, and on our skin. Usually this is a good thing. These microorganisms perform important tasks, like digesting the grilled cheese sandwich you ate for lunch. But sometimes, harmful microbes that cause disease are introduced into our bodies. Bacteria and protists are types of microbes.

CONTAGIOUS VERSUS INFECTIOUS

CONTAGIOUS MEANS A disease can be transmitted directly from human to human. *Infectious* means a disease can be transmitted directly *or* indirectly. An infectious germ can be transmitted from any source, including a bug.

If you have a cold, you are both infectious and contagious. If you sneeze, some of the cold virus you sneeze out could directly infect another person, if that person touches a surface you sneezed on, or shakes hands with you and you haven't washed your hands, or breathes in droplets of the virus you've just sneezed into the surrounding air.

However, some illnesses can be infectious without being contagious. Although many are life threatening, you can't catch them from another person. You only become ill if an insect bites a sick person and then bites you. You could theoretically sleep in the same bed with a yellow fever or bubonic plague or malaria victim and not catch yellow fever or plague or malaria, unless there's a diseased flea or mosquito in the room that bites you. Yellow fever, bubonic plague, and malaria are highly infectious but not contagious.

pandemic: A deadly epidemic that spreads quickly to lots of places.

parasite: In ancient Greece, it used to mean a professional dinner guest who flattered or amused the host. Now it means a creature that takes without giving. In scientific terms, parasites are organisms that survive only by living off a host. Some insects are parasites. Others transmit parasites from one person to another.

pathogen: An agent that causes disease, more commonly called a germ. A pathogen can be a bacterium, virus, or protist.

protist: Any organism that is not a plant, animal, or fungus. Protists are also tiny but are more complex than bacteria. Some protists transmitted by insects cause diseases such as malaria and sleeping sickness.

siege: To "lay siege" or "besiege" means to surround a walled city or castle and cut off supplies so that people will be forced to surrender.

vaccine: A weakened or killed version of a pathogen introduced as a method of preventing serious disease. If the real pathogen should show up later, the person's immune system will "remember" it and destroy it.

vector: A transmitter. Insects may act as vectors—transmitters—of many deadly diseases. Other animals can be vectors too, such as rodents, birds, and snails, but by far the most numerous transmitters of pathogens to humans are arthropods.

virus: Pathogens that are much tinier than bacteria and that don't feed or grow. To reproduce, a virus invades a living cell, hijacks it, and forces it to reproduce new viruses that can then invade other cells. Insect-borne viruses include yellow fever and encephalitis.

Further Reading and Surfing

BOOKS

Here are some books (asterisks denote books written for young readers) that may be of interest to serious students of bugs and history. See Notes on Sources for specific references.

Berenbaum, May R. *Bugs in the System: Insects and Their Impact on Human Affairs*. Reading, MA: Addison-Wesley, 1995.

Crosby, Molly Caldwell. *The American Plague: The Untold Story of Yellow Fever, the Epidemic That Shaped Our History*. New York: Berkley Books, 2006.

Dunn, John M. *Life during the Black Death*. San Diego: Lucent Books, 2000.

*Friedlander Jr., Mark P. *Outbreak: Disease Detectives at Work*. Minneapolis: Lerner Publications, 2000.

Greenfield, Amy Butler. *A Perfect Red: Empire, Espionage, and the Quest for the Color of Desire*. New York: HarperCollins, 2005.

*Jurmain, Suzanne. *The Secret of the Yellow Death: A True Story of Medical Sleuthing*. Boston: Houghton Mifflin, 2009.

Karlen, Arno. *Man and Microbes: Disease and Plagues in History and Modern Times.* New York: Putnam, 1995.

Mayor, Adrienne. *Greek Fire, Poison Arrows, and Scorpion Bombs: Biological and Chemical Warfare in the Ancient World.* Woodstock, NY: Overlook Press, 2009.

McNeill, William H. *Plagues and Peoples.* Garden City, NY: Anchor Books, 1976.

*Murphy, Jim. *An American Plague: The True and Terrifying Story of the Yellow Fever Epidemic of 1793.* New York: Clarion, 2003.

Rocco, Fiammetta. *The Miraculous Fever-Tree: Malaria and the Quest for a Cure That Changed the World.* New York: HarperCollins, 2003.

*Senior, Kathryn; illustrated by David Antram. *You Wouldn't Want to Be Sick in the 16th Century!* Danbury, CT: Franklin Watts, 2002.

Shah, Sonia. *The Fever: How Malaria Has Ruled Humankind for 500,000 Years.* New York: Sarah Crichton Books/Farrar, Straus and Giroux, 2010.

Simpson, Howard N. *Invisible Armies: The Impact of Disease on American History.* Indianapolis: Bobbs-Merrill, 1980.

*Waldbauer, Gilbert. *The Handy Bug Answer Book.* Detroit, MI: Visible Ink Press, 1998.

Zimmer, Carl. *Parasite Rex: Inside the Bizarre World of Nature's Most Dangerous Creatures.* New York: Free Press, 2000.

Zinsser, Hans. *Rats, Lice and History: Being a Study in Biography, Which, after Twelve Preliminary Chapters Indispensable for the Preparation of the Lay Reader, Deals with the Life History of Typhus Fever.* Boston: Printed and pub. for the Atlantic Monthly Press by Little, Brown, and Co., 1935.

WEBSITES

General Info

www.nationalgeographic.com

http://discovermagazine.com

http://kids.sandiegozoo.org/animals/insects

Insect Info

www.insects.org
A great kid-friendly website about insects, including a bug of the week.

www.entsoc.org
At the Entomological Society of America website, you can find insect-related resources, including FAQs, great insect collections, and identification services. Click on "about entomology/resources for the public."

Many zoos and natural history museums have great bug collections:

www.amnh.org American Museum of Natural History in New York

http://fieldmuseum.org The Field Museum in Chicago

www.nhm.org Natural History Museum of Los Angeles County

www.mnh.si.edu Smithsonian National Museum of Natural History in Washington, DC. (Their entomology page is at: www.entomology.si.edu)

Insect ID

www.npwrc.usgs.gov
At the Northern Prairie Wildlife Research Center site you can click on "Insects/Invertebrates" for great ID tools and additional resources to check out.

Diseases Transmitted by Insects

www.cdc.gov
Visit the Centers for Disease Control and Prevention and search insect-transmitted diseases for information and updates.

www.who.int

The World Health Organization website monitors disease outbreaks and provides updates about progress fighting many insect-transmitted diseases.

http://cartercenter.org

Visit the Carter Center website for information about fighting many of the insect-borne diseases mentioned in this book that afflict people in developing countries today. (Click on "Health Programs.")

www.epa.gov

The US Environmental Protection Agency website has resources for students and a state-by-state listing of environment agencies and other great resources.

Information about Insect Pests

www.askthebugman.com

For safe and sensible pest management advice, blog posts about bugs, and all sorts of cool and fascinating questions you hadn't even thought to ask, go to Richard Fagerlund's "ask the Bugman" site.

www.epa.gov/opp00001/factsheets/ipm.htm

Almost every state has an integrated pest management program, which is a low-toxicity approach to controlling pests. Visit the EPA's Integrated Pest Management resource page at the website above, or Google [your state] plus "IPM."

www.panna.org

The Pesticide Action Network is a site that discusses alternatives to pesticides worldwide.

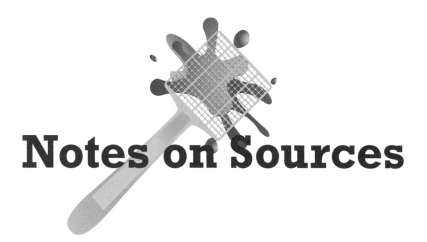

Notes on Sources

Chapter One

The statistic that there are three hundred pounds of insects for each pound of us comes from an article by Natalie Angier in the *New York Times* (February 18, 1991), which can be found online at www.nytimes.com/1991/02/18/movies/what-s-creepy-crawly-and-big-in-movies-bugs.html?pagewanted=all&src=pm. The idea that the plagues of Egypt are bug-based comes from Berenbaum (page 194), as does the general info about insects' ability to reproduce, numbers of locusts, and insect size (page 111). The information about epidemic diseases happening to impoverished people comes from Zimmer (page 203).

Chapter Two

Fossilized nits found on mummies is described in Berenbaum (page 202). The story of Thomas à Becket is recounted by Michael Batterberry and Ariane Ruskin Batterberry in *Mirror, Mirror: A Social History of Fashion* (New York: Holt, Rinehart and Winston, 1977, page 81).

Chapter Three

The story of the empress and silk is recounted in Batterberry and Batterberry (page 57). Information about lac insects and products is found in Berenbaum (pages 120–121), and how lac is made is described in Waldbauer (page 241). The history of cochineal is recounted in Greenfield (pages 3–4, 41–44). Beeswax information is from Waldbauer (page 241). A good article about zombie bees, "'Zombie' Fly Parasite Killing Honeybees" by Katherine Harmon Courage, can be found at Observations, Scientific American Blog Network (http://blogs.scientificamerican.com/observations/2012/01/03/zombie-fly-parasite-killing-honeybees/).

The recipe for Chocolate-Covered Crickets is adapted from Aletheia Price, "Eating Bugs!" (*Manataka American Indian Council*, http://www.manataka.org/page160.html). A historical account of maggot therapy comes from Larry Dossey, *The Extraordinary Healing Power of Ordinary Things: Fourteen Natural Steps to Health and Happiness* (New York: Random House Digital, Inc., 2007, e-book page 160). The cockroach living without its head is described in an article by Charles Choi in *Scientific American* called "Fact or Fiction? A Cockroach Can Live without Its Head," March 15, 2007 (http://www.scientific american.com/article.cfm?id=fact-or-fiction-cockroach-can-live-without-head). The healing power of cockroach brains is from an article in *National Geographic* online called "Cockroach Brains May Hold New Antibiotics?" by Christine Dell'Amore, published September 9, 2010 (http://nationalgeographic.com/news/2010/09/100909-cockroach-brains-mrsa-ecoli-antibiotics-science-health/). Forensic entomology and how a dead body is colonized comes from Josie Glausiusz and Volker Steger, *Buzz: The Intimate Bond Between Humans and Insects* (San Francisco: Chronicle Books, 2004, page 102), and also from Zakaria Erzinçlioğlu, *Maggots, Murder, and Men: Memories and Reflections of a Forensic Entomologist* (New York: Thomas Dunne Books, 2002, page 204). Insects in garments is from Frank Cowan, *Curious Facts in the History of Insects* (Philadelphia: J. B. Lippincott & Co., 1865, page 54).

Chapter Four
Exsanguination is from "Pests of Medical Importance" by John R. Meyer, North Carolina State University (http://www.cals.ncsu.edu/course/ent425/text18/medical.html). Symptoms of plague comes from Berenbaum (page 213). Beehives in warfare comes from Mayor (pages 177–179), as does the information about the toxic beetles (pages 73–74). Information about how the Canadian north is largely uninhabited, as well as how insects have determined the movement of African tribes, is from Erzinçlioğlu (page 204), and also from David Quammen, *Natural Acts* (New York: Nick Lyons Books/Schocken Books, 1985), as quoted in Jeffrey Alan Lockwood, *Six-Legged Soldiers: Using Insects as Weapons of War* (Oxford: Oxford University Press, 2009, page 36). Schmidt published his pain index in 1984 and later revised it: J. O. Schmidt, "Hymenoptera Venoms: Striving Toward the Ultimate Defense Against Vertebrates," in *Insect Defenses: Adaptive Mechanisms and Strategies of Prey and Predators*, eds. D. Evans and J. O. Schmidt (Albany, NY: SUNY Press, 1990, pages 387–419). For more samplings of descriptions from his pain scale, you can go to Richard Conniff, "Stung," Living World, *Discover* Magazine, June 1, 2003 (http://discovermagazine.com/2003/jun/featstung#.UPQ1ubam6I0).

Chapter Five
The information about crowd diseases comes from Karlen (page 57) and Zinsser (page 89); the information about endemic diseases and parents conferring immunity to their children is from Karlen (page 57), and diagnosing diseases of the past is also from Karlen (page 56).

Chapter Six
Sanskrit and Chinese documents on malaria and ancient Indian and Chinese fever gods comes

from McNeill (page 79). Information about Philistines and Israelites is from James Ronald Busvine, *Insects, Hygiene and History* (London: Athlone Press, 1976, page 57), and about emerods is from Zinsser (pages 109–110) as well as Karlen (page 55). The story of Sennacherib leaving Judea alone comes from an essay, "Infectious Alternatives: The Plague that Saved Jerusalem, 701 BC," by William H. McNeill, in *What If? The World's Foremost Military Historians Imagine What Might Have Been*, ed. Robert Cowley (New York: G. P. Putnam's Sons, 1999). The plague of Athens comes from Karlen (pages 59–60) and Zinsser (pages 120–123), and the comparison between the Roman and Chinese empires is from McNeill (page 93). The epidemic of ancient Rome information comes from McNeill (page 104), Karlen (page 71), and Zinsser (pages 135–139). Malaria in ancient Rome comes from Shah (page 68). Attila information is from Zinsser (pages 142–144) and Karlen (pages 72–75). The plague of Justinian is from Karlen (pages 74–75), Zinsser (pages 144–146), and McNeill (page 113). The stealing of silkworm eggs comes from Batterberry (page 68).

Chapter Seven

The idea of empires shifting from the Mediterranean and of a relatively disease-free time comes from Karlen (page 80), and the information on crusader diseases comes from Zinsser (pages 155–158). The origin of bubonic plague comes from McNeill (page 133) and Friedlander (page 37). What Mongols ate is detailed in Richard A. Gabriel, *Subotai the Valiant: Genghis Khan's Greatest General* (Westport, CT: Praeger, 2004, page 36). Wolves wandering through towns is from Friedlander (page 39); ghost ships is from Karlen (page 89); and throwing money over walls is from Dunn (page 50).

Chapter Eight

Bleeding information is from J. L. Turk and E. Allen, "Bleeding and Cupping," *Annals of the Royal College of Surgeons of England* 65, 1983 (pages 128–131). Battle in Grenada comes from Karlen (pages 114–115) and Zinsser (pages 241–245). Conquistadores and disease is from Karlen (pages 97–105); so few diseases in the New World comes from Karlen (page 100). Cortés and other conquistador stories are from McNeill (pages 180–183).

Chapter Nine

Fire ants in Hispaniola comes from "Solving the Mystery of Centuries-Old Plagues" by Alvin Powell, *Harvard Gazette–Harvard Public Affairs & Communications*. (http://www.news.harvard.edu/gazette/2005/02.03/05-ant.html), and also from Edward O. Wilson, "Environment: Early Ant Plagues in the New World," *Nature* 433, January 6, 2005, page 32, doi:10.1038/433032a; published online January 5, 2005. The origins of the slave trade and the introduction of yellow fever and malaria to the New World is from Karlen (pages 105–107). Insects in Africa and the problems with colonization come from Shah (page 38) and Simpson (page 20). Bantus' resistance to disease comes from Shah (page 35) and from ed. Kenneth F. Kiple, *The Cambridge World History of Human Disease* (New York: Cambridge University Press, 1993, page 295).

Chapter Ten

Spain on the wane comes from McNeill (page 152). English settlers comes from Karlen (page 107) and Shah (pages 39–41). Distrust of cinchona is from Friedlander (pages 58–59). Spanish click beetles story is from Lt. John T. Ambrose, "Insects in Warfare," *Army*, December 1974. The stories of plague families locked inside their houses comes from: http://www.britainexpress.com/History/plague.htm. Killer bees is from Berenbaum (pages 90–96).

Chapter Eleven

Disease during the Revolutionary War comes from Simpson (pages 110–117, 136) and from Gerald N. Callahan, *Infection: The Uninvited Universe* (New York: St. Martin's Press, 2006, page 172). The quote from young George Washington comes from Zinsser (page 187). The Hessian fly information comes from Waldbauer (page 260). Presidential bugs is from "Presidential Diseases," *Health in Plain English* (www.healthinplainenglish.com/presidential-diseases/index.htm). Disinfecting Hamilton is from Michael B. A. Oldstone, *Viruses, Plagues, and History* (New York: Oxford University Press, 1998, page 47).

Chapter Twelve

Haiti, Toussaint-Louverture, and Napoleon are from Robert K. D. Peterson, "Insects, Disease, and Military History: The Napoleonic Campaigns and Historical Perception," *American Entomologist*, Fall 1995 (pages 154–155), as well as Napoleon in Russia (pages 155–158). More on Napoleon's army is in Karlen (page 116) and Zinsser (pages 161–164). Lewis and Clark expedition and Rush's Bilious Pills are from "Rush's Bilious Pills," *Discovering Lewis & Clark: Home* (http://lewis-clark.org/content/content article.asp?ArticleID=2564). Pests Go West, and Boston and Michigan stats, are from Simpson (pages 38, 172). Info on Boston's life expectancy is from Oscar Handlin, *Boston's Immigrants [1790–1880]; A Study in Acculturation,* rev. and enl. ed. (Cambridge, MA: Belknap Press of Harvard University Press, 1959, page 114). The information from Darwin's account of being bitten by assassin bugs comes from Chapter XV: Passage Of The Cordillera, March 25, 1835, *Charles Darwin–Free Online Library* (http://darwin.thefreelibrary.com/The-Voyage-of-the-Beagle/15-1-2). Death by Bug and ants' nests come from *International Wildlife Encyclopedia* by Maurice Burton and Robert Burton (Tarrytown, NY: Marshall Cavendish, 2002, third ed., vol. 1, page 92); from Will Durant, *Our Oriental Heritage* (New York: Simon and Schuster, 1963, page 362); and also from Lockwood (page 36).

Chapter Thirteen

Information about the potato blight comes from Karlen (pages 116–121) and from Zinsser (pages 161–164), and about Irish in British workhouses from Joseph Conlon, "The Historical Impact of Epidemic Typhus" (http://entomology.montana.edu/historybug/typhus-conlon.pdf). Nightingale and the Crimean War is from Florence Nightingale, *Encyclopedia of World Biography* (www.notablebiographies.com). Stories of bugs during the Civil War come from Rocco (pages 174, 178), Shah (page 73), and from Gary L. Miller: "Historical Natural History: Insects and the Civil War," *American Entomologist* 43, Winter 1997 (pages 227–245). Dr. Black Vomit is from Lockwood (page 76) and Crosby (page 109). Trouvelot and gypsy moths comes from Ronald M. Weseloh, "People and the Gypsy Moth: A Story of Human Interactions with an Invasive Species," *American Entomologist* 49, no. 3, Fall 2003 (pages 180–190). Information on locust plagues is from "When the Skies Turned to Black: The Locust Plague of 1875," by *Hearthstone Legacy Publication* (www.hearthstonelegacy.com), and also Katherine Harmon, "When Grasshoppers Go Biblical: Serotonin Causes Locusts to Swarm," in *Scientific American, Science News, Articles and Information/Scientific American* (http://www.scientificamerican.com/article.cfm?id=when-grasshoppers-go-bibl). Crash course comes from John Roach, "Locusts Inspire Technology That May Prevent Car Crashes," *Daily Nature and Science News and Headlines/ National Geographic News* (http://news.nationalgeographic.com/news/2004/08/0806_040806_locusts.html).

Chapter Fourteen

Information about Yersin and Kitasato is from Myron J. Echenberg, *Plague Ports: The Global Urban Impact of Bubonic Plague, 1894–1901* (New York: New York University Press, 2007, page 35), as well as Busvine (pages 231–232). Bombay plague is from Echenberg (page 15). The idea that coffee might have antimalarial properties comes from Shah (97—see footnote 24). Spanish-American War diseases comes from Waldbauer (page 257). Charles Ledger information is from Friedlander (pages 58–59). British Invasion is from Shah (page 89). Artemisinin is from Shah (pages 112–120). Laveran, Ross, Grassi comes from Shah (pages 144–146, 152–160) and from Rossi (chapter 9). Reed Commission information is from *Claude Moore Health Sciences* (www.hsl.virginia.edu/historical/medical_history/yellow_fever/impact.cfm). Information about workers swatting mosquitoes and not being protected comes from: hsl.virginia.edu; Friedlander (pages 57–58); and also Shah (page 183). Blacks died as easily as whites, lacking immunity, is from Karlen (page 108). Information about William Gorgas (and being called Dr. Gorgeous) comes from Shah (page 179) and from Rocco (pages 200–205). Information about cigars and whiskey for yellow fever comes from Shah (page 179). Panama volunteers comes from Rocco (page 201) as well as Indian army and gin and tonic (page 205); prejudiced time comes from Shah (page 183).

Chapter Fifteen

Information about the World War I typhus epidemic is from Zinsser (pages 299–301). Soldiers on the eastern front using blister beetles comes from Lockwood (page 78). Some information about the boll weevil comes from James C. Giesen, *Boll Weevil Blues: Cotton, Myth, and Power in the American South* (Chicago: University of Chicago Press, 2011), especially the intro, ix–xii. CDC history is from Friedlander (page 58). The quinine crisis is from Friedlander (pages 58–59).

Chapter Sixteen

"Deadly to insects, but harmless to man . . ." is from Waldemar Kaempffert, "DDT, the Army's Insect Powder, Strikes a Blow Against Typhus and for Pest Control," *New York Times*, June 4, 1944. Arsenic, Paris green, lead arsenate, pyrethrum, DDT is from Edmund Russell, *War and*

Nature: Fighting Humans and Insects with Chemicals from World War I to Silent Spring (Cambridge: Cambridge University Press, 2001, pages 5–6). Beehive hairdos is from Lockwood (page 155). Rachel Carson and DDT/fire ants comes from Elizabeth Kolbert, "Human Nature," *The New Yorker*, May 28, 2007 (http://www.newyorker.com/talk/comment/2007/05/28/070528taco_talk_kolbert). Concentration of pesticides is from Suzanne Merkelson "Pesticides Linked to ADHD," TheAtlantic.com (http://www.theatlantic.com/technology/archive/2010/05/pesticides-linked-to-adhd/56831/). Potato beetles in World War II comes from Glausiusz (page 95).

Chapter Seventeen

Potatoes and pesticides is from Richie Chevat and Michael Pollan, *The Omnivore's Dilemma: The Secrets Behind What You Eat*, young readers ed. (New York: Dial Books, 2009, page 2). Information about ivermectin is from Zimmer (page 206). Biological control of leishmaniasis comes from Rebecca Kolberg, "Finding 'Sustainable' Ways to Prevent Parasitic Diseases," *Science* 264.5167 (1994): 1859 (Gale). Cockroaches on *Apollo 12* is from Josie Glausiusz, "Bzzzzzzzz: Why Insects are Vital to Human Survival" (Discovermagazine.com/2004/jun/bzzzzzzzz/article). Cassava case study is from Zimmer (pages 220–228). Zombie cockroaches is from "'Zombie' Roaches Lose Free Will Due to Wasp Venom" (news.nationalgeographic.com/news/2007/12/071206-roach-zombie_2.html). Grasshoppers information is from "Suicide Grasshoppers Brainwashed by Parasite Worms" (http://news.nationalgeographic.com/news/2005/09/0901_050901_worm parasite.html). Zombie fire ant comes from Thomas H. Maugh II, "Latest pest-control attempt: Turn fire ants into zombies," *LA Times*, May 16, 2009 (http://articles.latimes.com/2009/may/16/science/sci-zombieants16). Kinder, gentler parasites is from Zimmer (page 212), and lay and display is also from Zimmer (page 213). Worm therapy comes from "Scientists at Work/David Pritchard: The Worms Crawl In," by Elizabeth Svoboda, *New York Times*, July 1, 2008 (http://www.nytimes.com/2008/07/01/health/research/01prof.html?_r=2&ref=science&oref=slogin&), and also from Zimmer (pages 213–215). Termite tower information is from Jill Fehrenbacher, "Biomimetic Architecture: Green Building in Zimbabwe Modeled After Termite Mounds," November 29, 2012 (http://inhabitat.com/building-modelled-on-termites-eastgate-centre-in-zimbabwe).

Acknowledgments

I am grateful to many people for their help with this book. My niece, Dara Strauss-Albee, who possesses 98 percent of my family's science aptitude and is now a PhD candidate in immunology at the Stanford University School of Medicine, read and helped me revise many of the sciencey sections of the book, as did my good friend Laura Monti, scientist and revered teacher of AP biology, who practically dictated the glossary to me.

Thanks also to Professor Melissa Perry of the Department of Environmental and Occupational Health in George Washington University's School of Public Health and Health Services; Dr. Melody Palmore, Assistant Professor of Infectious Disease at the Emory University School of Medicine; and Dr. James Kuhn, of Portland, Maine, all of whom graciously answered my many questions related to pesticides, germs, and infectious diseases. Dr. Paul Sax, Clinical Director of the Division of Infectious Diseases and the HIV Program at Brigham and Women's Hospital, and Associate Professor of Medicine at Harvard, gets extra-special thanks for having read and critiqued lengthy sections of the manuscript for accuracy.

Jonathan Losos, Professor of Organismic and Evolutionary Biology at Harvard, and also my long-time friend and go-to expert on all things zoological, was most helpful on the subject of malaria prophylaxis.

Any errors are mine, not those of my scientist and doctor experts.

I'm also grateful to my good friends and fellow writers Michaela Muntean and Marcia DeSanctis for reading and critiquing the manuscript, to the awesome librarians at the Taft School for their ongoing help ordering mounds of interlibrary loan materials for me, and to scientist-photographers Michel Lecoq, Kathy Keatley Garvey, and Christopher Quock for gracious permission to use their amazing photos.

Thanks also to illustrator Robert Leighton for his hilarious cartoons; my wonderful agent, Caryn Wiseman; my excellent editor, Emily Easton; and to the Society of Children's Writers and Illustrators.

And lastly, a big thanks to my husband, Jon, and to my children, Sam, Cassie, and Luke, for their love and support as this book inched and skittered its way to publication.

Picture Credits

page ii: U.S. National Archives and Records Administration/Wikimedia Commons; **page iii:** The George F. Landegger Collection of Alabama Photographs in Carol M. Highsmith's America, Library of Congress, Prints and Photographs Division; **page 2:** © Universal International Pictures/Photofest; **page 3:** S.V. Scary Films 2 Inc. and Outrage Productions 4 Inc.; **page 4:** Clinton & Charles Robertson, Del Rio, TX, and College Station, TX/Wikimedia Commons; **page 6:** © BijouFlix Releasing/Photofest; **page 9:** Mary Evans Picture Library/David Lewis Hodgson; **page 10:** Mike R/Wikimedia Commons; **page 12:** courtesy of the National Library of Medicine; **page 13:** Gianreali/Wikimedia Commons; **page 15:** Joseph Martin Kronheim/Wikimedia Commons; **page 16:** © topseller/Shutterstock: **page 17 (top):** © Suzan Oschmann/Shutterstock; **page 17 (bottom):** © holbox/Shutterstock; **page 18:** Jeffrey W. Lotz, Florida Department of Agriculture and Consumer Services, Bugwood.org; **page 19:** Mary Evans Picture Library/Edwin Mullan Collection; **page 20:** © Africa Studio/Shutterstock; **page 22 (top):** © Christopher Quock; **page 22 (bottom):** © swissmacky/Shutterstock; **page 23:** © Eric R. Day, Virginia Polytechnic Institute and State University, Bugwood.org; **page 24:** courtesy of the National Library of Medicine; **page 25:** © Kathy Keatley Garvey; **page 26:** © Studiotouch/Shutterstock; **page 27:** JJ Harrison/Wikimedia Commons; **page 29:** James Gathany/courtesy CDC; **page 30:** courtesy of the National Library of Medicine; **page 31:** courtesy of the National Library of Medicine; **page 32 (top and bottom):** courtesy of the National Library of Medicine; **page 34:** Merle Shepard, Gerald R.Carner, and P.A.C Ooi, Insects and their Natural Enemies Associated with Vegetables and Soybean in Southeast Asia, Bugwood.org; **page 35:** © IndianSummer/Shutterstock; **page 36:** Jerry A. Payne, USDA Agricultural Research Service, Bugwood.org; **page 41:** © Starkblast/iStockphoto.com; **page 42:** Rafael Brix/Wikimedia Commons; **page 43:** courtesy of the National Library of Medicine; **page 44:** Matanya/Wikimedia Commons; **page 46:** Marie-Lan Nguyen/Wikimedia Commons; **page 47:** National Gallery of Art, Washington, DC; gift of Therese K. Straus; **page 48:** © Marcin-linfernum/Shutterstock; **page 50:** Mary Evans Picture Library; **page 52:** Marie-Lan Nguyen/Wikimedia Commons; **page 53:** INTERFOTO/NG Collection/Mary Evans; **page 54:** © Columbia Pictures/Photofest; **page 55:** © Andrey Burmakin/Shutterstock; **page 58:** courtesy of the Art Renewal Center (www.artrenewal.org); **page 59:** Pierre Grivolas/Wikimedia Commons; **page 61:** John Vanderlyn/Wikimedia Commons; **page 62:** courtesy of the National Library of Medicine; **page 63:** Pieter Claesz/Wikimedia Commons; **page 66:** courtesy of the Library of Congress; **page 67:** BrokenSphere/Wikimedia Commons; **page 68:** Pieter Claesz/Wikimedia Commons; **page 70 (top and bottom):** courtesy of the Library of Congress; **page 71:** National Gallery of Art, Washington, DC; Samuel H. Kress Collection; **page 73:** Turnbull FL/Wikimedia Commons; **page 76:** Wikimedia Commons; **page 78 (top):** Wikimedia Commons; **page 78 (bottom):** Jodocus Hondius/Wikimedia Commons; **page 79:** © I. Pilon/Shutterstock; **page 81:** J. Andrews/Wikimedia Commons; **page 85:** S.V. Scary Films 2 Inc. and Outrage Productions 4 Inc.; **page 87:** Wikimedia Commons; **page 88:** Scott Bauer/courtesy of USDA-ARS; **page 89:** courtesy of the National Library of Medicine; **page 91:** Wikimedia Commons; **page 92:** Wikimedia Commons; **page 93:** courtesy of the Library of Congress; **page 94 (left):** William Clark by Charles Willson Peale, from life, 1807–1808; courtesy of Independence National Historical Park; **page 94 (right):** Meriwether Lewis by Charles Willson Peale, from life, 1807; courtesy of Independence National Historical Park; **page 96:** © Maximus256/Shutterstock; **page 97:** courtesy of the Library of Congress; **page 98:** courtesy of the National Library of Medicine; **page 99:** J. Cameron/Wikimedia Commons; **page 101:** Wikimedia Commons; **page 102:** courtesy of the Library of Congress; **page 103:** Wikimedia Commons; **page 104:** courtesy of the National Library of Medicine; **page 105:** courtesy of the National Library of Medicine; **page 106:** courtesy of the Library of Congress; **page 108:** © Michel Lecoq; **page 110:** courtesy of the Library of Congress; **page 111 (top):** © Michael Taylor/Shutterstock; **page 111 (bottom left):** courtesy of the National Library of Medicine; **page 111 (bottom right):** KwanShanYuet/Wikimedia Commons; **page 112:** Wikimedia Commons; **page 113:** © Aleksandra Nadeina/Shutterstock; **page 114:** courtesy of the Library of Congress; **page 115:** Varges Ariel/Imperial War Museums; **page 116:** H. Zell/Wikimedia Commons; **page 117 (left and right):** courtesy of the National Library of Medicine; **page 118:** courtesy of the National Library of Medicine; **page 119:** courtesy of the National Library of Medicine; **page 120:** courtesy of the National Library of Medicine; **page 121 (top):** Wikimedia Commons; **page 121 (bottom):** courtesy of the Library of Congress; **page 122:** courtesy of the National Library of Medicine; **page 123:** Wikimedia Commons; **page 124:** World War I ad: "The Cleanest Fighter in the World—the British Tommy," author unknown; **page 125:** courtesy of the National Museum of Health and Medicine, Armed Forces Institute of Pathology, Washington, DC; **page 126:** courtesy of USDA-ARS; **page 127 (top and bottom):** courtesy of the National Library of Medicine; **page 129:** © Photofest; **page 130 (top):** Wikimedia Commons; **page 130 (bottom):** © Dudarev Mikhail/Shutterstock; **page 131 (top left):** Scott Bauer/courtesy of USDA-ARS; **page 131 (right):** Murray S. Blum, University of Georgia, Bugwood.org; **page 131 (bottom left):** Smithsonian Institution (http://siarchives.si.edu)/Wikimedia Commons; **page 133:** © Thomas Oswald/Shutterstock; **page 134 (top):** Clemson University—USDA Cooperative Extension Slide Series, Bugwood.org; **page 134 (bottom):** Laitche/Wikimedia Commons; **page 136:** courtesy CDC; **page 138:** courtesy malarianomore.org/uk; **page 140:** Walter Reed Army Institute of Research/courtesy of USDA-ARS; **page 141:** © Againsta/Shutterstock; **page 142 (top):** © tomka/Shutterstock; **page 142 (bottom):** Scott Bauer/courtesy of USDA-ARS; **page 144 (left):** Sanford D. Porter, USDA-ARS, Center for Medical, Agricultural and Veterinary Entomology, Bugwood.org; **page 144 (right):** Sanford Porter/Courtesy of USDA-ARS; **page 145:** State Archives of Florida; **page 146:** © Elnu/Shutterstock; **page 147 (left):** J Brew/Wikimedia Commons; **page 147 (right):** © Arup.

Index

Note: Page numbers in *italics* indicate illustrations.